INDIA
THEN & NOW

INDIA
THEN & NOW
~*An Insider's Account*~

BIMAL JALAN

Published by
Rupa Publications India Pvt. Ltd 2020
7/16, Ansari Road, Daryaganj
New Delhi 110002

Sales Centres:
Allahabad Bengaluru Chennai
Hyderabad Jaipur Kathmandu
Kolkata Mumbai

Copyright © Bimal Jalan 2020

The views and opinions expressed in this book are the author's own and the facts are as reported by him which have been verified to the extent possible, and the publishers are not in any way liable for the same.

All rights reserved.
No part of this publication may be reproduced, transmitted, or stored in a retrieval system, in any form or by any means, electronic, mechanical, photocopying, recording or otherwise, without the prior permission of the publisher.

ISBN: 978-93-5333-999-9

First impression 2020

10 9 8 7 6 5 4 3 2 1

Printed at Parksons Graphics Pvt. Ltd, Mumbai

The moral right of the author has been asserted.
This book is sold subject to the condition that it shall not, by way of trade or otherwise, be lent, resold, hired out, or otherwise circulated, without the publisher's prior consent, in any form of binding or cover other than that in which it is published.

CONTENTS

Preface   *vii*
Introduction   *ix*

Section I:
The Decade of Industrialization

1. The Story of India's Industrialization   3
2. The Quest for Self-Reliance   20
3. To Tax or Not to Tax   32
4. Saved by NRIs   45
5. Marching Towards a New Industrial Policy   53
6. Strategizing Development, Delivering Performance   63

Section II:
The Decade of Liberalization and Globalization

7. The Graph of India's Economy   73
8. Scientific Temper, Technological Strides   83
9. Of Quick Economic Turnarounds   92
10. Strategy Post Crisis   103
11. The Shifting Paradigm of Finance and Development   111
12. Management Challenges in a Global World   127

Section III:
India in the Twenty-First Century

13. The Economics of Exchange Rates   139
14. Is the Parliament Being Silenced?   152
15. Ethics in Banking   166
16. Politics and Governance   175
17. The Prosperity Paradox   183
18. The Future Is Ours   193

Index   203

PREFACE

As a witness to India's economic trajectory through the decades, I decided to put together for the readers my writings that reflect how India has progressed since Independence to the present times. In doing so, I was principally guided by two considerations: the first was to cover different subject areas that may be of interest to the general reader in addition to experts in economics, politics and administration. In the pages that follow, you will encounter my writings on the Indian economy, broader issues of development policy, emerging challenges for management, the role of science and technology, exchange-rate management, globalization, and so on. The second consideration was to make this volume relevant to the ongoing debate on India's approach to policy reforms as we move towards 2025 and beyond.

The task of preparing this volume and selecting papers of contemporary interest turned out to be much more difficult than I had originally anticipated. I am particularly grateful to Satish Choudhary for his hard work in preparing the manuscript for publication and to K.D. Sharma for his organizational and other help.

My special thanks to Rupa Publications for ensuring the timely publication of the book.

INTRODUCTION

The 18 chapters in this volume have been divided into three sections. These sections are both chronological and thematic in nature, as each of the separate periods covered by them invariably have distinct themes. The first section primarily deals with the 1970s, which was the decade of India's industrialization. At this point, the economy as a whole was highly controlled through industrial licencing policies and a plethora of legal and administrative bottlenecks. The post-Independence consensus was shaped by the colonial experience and the pre-War realities of trading and investment relationships between industrial and non-industrial countries. Both the factors—the colonial experience and the pre-War trade patterns—strongly favoured an inward-looking and State-dominated strategy of development. These issues are highlighted in the first chapter, 'The Story of India's Industrialization'. It is followed by the chapter, 'The Quest for Self-Reliance'. The subsequent chapters in Section I deal with some suggestions for a new industrial policy and overall development strategy for strengthening India's growth prospects. The primary message of the essays that make up Section I is essentially that improvement in India's growth prospects does not necessarily mean a decrease in the level of government or public control of economic activities; it simply means that the system of controls should produce demonstrable benefits in terms of the country's objectives. Administrative ability, no less than material resources, is scarce in developing countries, and it is necessary that it should be efficiently allocated. There is really no point in continuing with controls that cannot be properly administered.

Section II, 'The Decade of Liberalization and Globalization' focuses on the 1980s, when India's policy framework substantially shifted from a protectionist framework to liberalization and globalization in terms of trade and investment. Two particularly important chapters in this section are on economic management during a period of severe balance-of-payments crisis in 1988, and the need for a new economic strategy after the crisis in the early 1990s. The other chapters in this section attempt to provide perspectives on certain policy issues in respect of management of the financial system and challenges in a globalizing economy.

Before 1991, the role of the financial system in India was essentially limited, and allocations of resources were made by central planning authorities and not by the financial markets. This situation changed sharply in the 1990s when all the developing countries were moving towards a more market-determined strategy. At the same time, in light of the Asian crisis, it was also realized that financial markets had to be closely monitored by regulatory and supervisory agencies. Events in East Asia highlighted the two-way interaction between the financial sector and the development policies adopted by industrializing countries. As such, proper emphasis had to be placed on growth policies that do not give rise to problems that engender systemic instability in the financial sector (for example, because of a large fiscal deficit). Over time, India adopted international prudential norms and practices with regard to capital adequacy, credit delivery, income and provisioning requirement by banks. Prudent limits were also placed on the financial system and the corporate sector's external borrowings.

In the 1990s, India cautiously but systematically moved from a comprehensive control regime to current account convertibility (CAC) and market-determined exchange rate. Short-term debt was carefully monitored, with differential treatment between trade- and non trade-related debt, and was subject to a quantitative ceiling. Deposits by non-resident Indians (NRIs) were also controlled through specification of interest rates or interest rate ceilings for different maturities. On the whole, India's management of the financial system was generally accepted by international institutions, particularly the World Bank and the International Monetary Fund (IMF), who extended help as and when required to cover balance-of-payments deficits.

The chapter on 'Management Challenges in a Global World' highlights the policies adopted by India to handle the problems associated with dismantling of the industrial licencing and control system that was prevalent for several decades after Independence. As a result of liberalization of the domestic economy and reduction of domestic protection through lowering of tariffs, the industrial sector was exposed to both internal and external competition. India was able to manage these challenges by launching policies to encourage the industrial sector to take maximum advantage of technology, technical skills and cost-competitiveness. Over time, a perceptible difference was noticed in the attitude of entrepreneurs and managers in giving importance to consumer preferences, forward-looking planning and devising firm-specific strategies to improve their shares in domestic and international markets.

Compared to the historical trend, the impact of these policies was positive and significant. The growth rate of the economy during 1992–3 to 1999–2000 was close to 6.5 per cent per annum. The balance-of-payments position also improved.

Current account deficits were moderate, while India's external debt (as a percentage of the Gross Domestic Product [GDP]) and debt-servicing burden actually came down since the early 1990s. There was also evidence of considerable restructuring in the corporate sector, with attention being given to cost-competitiveness and financial viability.

Section III centres on 'India in the Twenty-First Century'. Here, the chapters cover selected issues on India's economics, politics and governance in the first quarter of the twenty-first century. India is the world's largest democracy, with free and fair elections held every five years (or more frequently, if required). Its reputation as the fastest-growing economy in the twenty-first century has been highly appreciated and it has become a role model for the other developing countries. In terms of governance structure as well, the period 2000–19 was very different from the earlier period of 1980–2000. During 2000–14, there were three governments with full terms in office. However, none of these governments—two formed by the Congress, and one by the National Democratic Alliance (NDA)—had majorities of their own and were supported by coalitions of several small parties. As such, it became very difficult for any government to introduce basic reforms or change governance structure.

In the last five years, from 2014 to 2019, for the first time, India has had the advantage of a government with a majority of its own and has been in a position to introduce several basic reforms that have been pending for a long time. For example, the government introduced Goods and Services Tax (GST) which, despite some hiccups, is one of the most significant reforms in India's economic history since Independence. Several other positive measures were also taken, such as the disbursement of subsidies to the poor through Direct Benefit Transfer (DBT), significant increase in public investments in infrastructure, increasing foreign direct investment (FDI) inflows, labour reforms and launch of the 'Digital India' campaign.

The first chapter in this section, 'The Economics of Exchange Rates', deals with exchange-rate management, an issue that is as relevant today as it was in the earlier years of this century. Currently, there is a fair amount of discussion in the media about the policy being followed by the Reserve Bank of India (RBI) in managing the exchange rate in the global context. Over time, by 2003, India's foreign exchange reserves increased substantially, and are now one of the largest among developing countries. The fact that most of the constituents of India's balance of payments in the twenty-first century are showing positive trends is a reflection of the increasing competitiveness of the Indian economy and the strong confidence of the international community in India's growth potential. Over time, India's policies on foreign exchange management in light of the Asian crisis have converged around some universally accepted views. Among these are: (i) exchange rates should be flexible and not fixed or pegged; (ii) countries should be able to intervene or manage exchange rates to at least some degree, if market movements are destabilizing in the short run and (iii) reserves should be sufficient to take care of fluctuations in capital flows and 'liquidity at risk'.

The next chapter, 'Is the Parliament Being Silenced?' highlights the diminishing role of Parliament in the conduct of national affairs. In the annals of India's long and distinguished parliamentary history, the events that took place over the five-day period from 18 March to 22 March during the Budget session of 2006 were quite unique. The government announced a number of unexpected decisions pertaining to the business agenda of the two Houses, which both the Houses readily accepted without any debate. The decisions involved a major change in the established procedure for consideration of the Budget, a drastic revision in the business of the two Houses without adequate notice and a sudden adjournment of Parliament sine die (followed by a reversal of this decision again a few days later). The passive and ready acceptance by Parliament, the supreme institution of India's democracy, of these decisions was contrary to well-established parliamentary conventions.

There have also been occasions when the silences of Parliament have been just as loud as the debates on foreign policy, employment and development policy. Generally, the tolerance for deviation from established norms and propriety is most evident when there is a clash of interest among different parties in search of political power after elections (or an adverse judicial verdict). During the Emergency in 1975–7, we had witnessed one of most conspicuous instances of such silences, when violations of established laws and administrative norms were either tolerated or approved through legislative amendments, including Constitutional amendments. Fortunately for India's democracy, such occasions have been relatively infrequent.

The chapter on 'Ethics in Banking' emphasizes the importance of an efficient regulatory system at the level of the central bank. It is of utmost importance that there is complete transparency and accountability of banks in respect of depositors' money. There is a need to ensure that actions taken by banks conform to international norms and regulatory guidelines, and there is public disclosure of their lending operations, particularly for granting benefits to large corporate borrowers by way of rescheduling loans, and so on.

In addition to ethics in banking, this chapter also deals with ethics in public policy formulation. The central message of the vast literature available on what may be considered to be ethical or unethical is that it depends largely on the circumstances. There are three definitive conclusions in this respect, which are independent of the context:

(i) Adherence to the 'Rule of Law' in a democratic society is an essential minimum requirement of ethical behaviour;
(ii) Any measure or policy decision that improves the welfare of some without causing harm to anyone else can be considered to be 'ethical' and
(iii) Public policy by the government in power should be designed to promote the 'greatest good for the greatest number'.

The chapter on 'Politics and Governance' highlights the fact that while India's opportunities and capabilities were comparatively large in the twenty-first century, it is also true that actual performance in alleviating poverty and providing minimum essential social services to the people was relatively low. In terms of Human Development Index (HDI), computed by the United Nations Development Programme (UNDP), India's rank in 2011 was 134 among 187 countries. Several political and governance reforms that are desirable for the new government to launch in the next few years in order to increase India's rank in HDI are discussed in the chapter on 'Politics and Governance'. These include reducing the built-in incentive for fragmentation of parties to take advantage of the anti-defection law, reducing the attractiveness of politics as a career of choice for persons with criminal records, eliminating the politicization of India's bureaucracy, delegating management of policies announced by the government or poverty alleviation to public-sector agencies, and so on.

As mentioned earlier, India's progress in providing social services to the poor has been relatively weak over the years.

After Independence, an overriding priority of the national government, as it has been of all governments since then, was to expand physical facilities to provide basic social services like education, health and nutrition to all sections of the population, particularly to the poor. However, a number of field surveys have revealed that implementation of social programmes launched by the Central and state governments have generally favoured the not-so-poor sections of the society. The chapter on 'The Prosperity Paradox' analyses India's performance in social sectors and discusses some policy issues, including the pattern of the government's budgetary expenditure on social services.

Compared with other items of expenditure in the Budget, the expenditure on social services by the Centre and states has been relatively low over time. It remained around 6 per cent of the GDP from 2012 to 2016. In addition to increasing social expenditure, while at the same time reducing fiscal deficits, it is suggested that there are three general principles that should be observed in the organization of social services. These are: (i) the need to prioritize allocations for the benefit of the poor; (ii) give cash 'vouchers' to the poor so that they can use these for the required goods and services and (iii) involve non-governmental organizations (NGOs) in the disbursement of funds in rural and semi-urban areas. The chapter also provides some suggestions on how to maximize benefits to the poorer sections in respect of priority areas of social importance, such as food, literacy and health.

The last chapter titled 'The Future Is Ours' deals with some long-term reforms that the government can initiate in the next few months during its second term, and which may be fully implemented in the next two to three years. In handling some of the long-term issues, one great advantage that India now has is that its economic fundamentals are very strong, perhaps better than at any time in the past 30 years. Looking ahead, an important reform is to launch a programme to drastically simplify the governance system at the ministerial and bureaucratic level. It is suggested that, with the exception of selected areas such as defence and security, it is desirable to cut through elaborate red tape and rely primarily on 'self-certification' by companies in both private and public sectors. A related area is to have total transparency in the decision-making process within the government. An important step in this direction should be to make it mandatory for all ministries and departments of the government to voluntarily make information, on the decisions taken by them available to the public directly, through media and/or through the ministerial website.

It is also desirable to reduce the political powers of ministers and their vested interests in the allocation of public resources. While the present system is theoretically sound, over time, there has been substantial erosion in the ability of Parliament/legislatures to hold ministers responsible, either collectively or individually, for the decisions taken by them. An important priority for the future is to ensure that any annual targets announced by a ministry are carefully reviewed for their feasibility in implementation.

In order to simplify administrative procedure, it is also necessary to substantially reduce the large number of persons who are hired as civil servants across a large number of ministries to implement policies announced by them. In order to facilitate this process, the government should also announce that all administrative staff currently employed will remain in office with full pensions, and also permit staff members to seek early retirement.

In order to reduce the present built-in incentive for fragmentation of parties in the Lok Sabha, it is of utmost importance that the so-called 'anti-defection law' is made applicable to all parties, and not only to the elected individuals of a party. At present, in the Lok Sabha with 543 members, a party with only 10 or 15 members (or even less) can join the government and enjoy ministerial berths.

Another important priority is to redefine the primary role of the government in the economy. Despite some important measures to liberalize domestic and international control in respect of production and trade, India still remains one of the most heavily regulated economies in the world. In fact, over time, despite liberalization, the role of the government (including state governments) has expanded in all spheres of the economy. All the announced policies that different ministries are supposed to handle, in association with other concerned ministries, take an enormous amount of time to be implemented on the ground, particularly in rural and underdeveloped areas, with substantial diversion of funds at different levels of the government at the Centre, states and districts.

Now that India has a government that has a substantial majority in Parliament in its second term, at the macroeconomic level, it should take policy measures to ensure a stable and competitive environment with a strong external sector and a transparent domestic administrative system. Implementation of policies announced by the government should be left to autonomous regulatory and promotional agencies. At the same time, the government's role in managing commercial enterprises deserves to be correspondingly reduced.

As mentioned in the final chapter, this is a relatively short list of agendas for the future for the re-elected government. If these policy reforms are successfully launched over the next three to four years, India's record in growth as well as poverty alleviation will substantially improve over time.

SECTION I

THE DECADE OF INDUSTRIALIZATION

1
THE STORY OF INDIA'S INDUSTRIALIZATION

The 1950s and 1960s saw manufacturing production in developing countries increase by about 7 per cent a year. Historically, this was unprecedented. Not only was this rate higher than in the past, it was also better than what many of the developed countries were able to achieve during the same period. However, while industrialization had helped in overcoming poverty, it had also created its own set of problems: it had led to increasing economic and social inequalities, regional disparities, widespread waste of resources, periodic balance-of-payments crises, dependence on aid, and so on.

The process of industrialization of developing countries was still in its infancy. While some countries had been longer at it than others, all of them still had far to go before they could be considered industrialized nations. No convincing answers could be found yet to the questions that most developing countries were grappling with: how to speed up the industrialization process and what kind of industries to promote, in what time sequence and with what kinds of instruments.

In considering such questions, an evaluation of past experiences could be a valuable guide, and development economists owe a debt of gratitude to the Development

Centre of the Organisation for Economic Co-operation and Development (OECD) for having provided an interesting survey of industrialization policies and results for the period. As part of the OECD survey, seven countries—Argentina, Brazil, Mexico, India, Pakistan, Taiwan and the Philippines—were studied by one or two economists with close first-hand knowledge of the country concerned. In addition to the country studies, the editors of the series—Ian Little, Tibor Scitovsky and Maurice Scott—undertook a comparative study of the industrialization experience.

Here, the comparative study and the three country studies on Mexico, Brazil and Pakistan are covered. The country studies essentially dealt with the progress of the countries, and reviewed the policy instruments chosen by them and the impact these policies had on the pattern of industrialization of each country. All three countries had been successful: Mexico achieved a growth rate of 6 per cent per annum over three decades (from the 1940s to 1960s); Brazil grew at an average rate of 6 per cent until the early 1960s; and Pakistan, after a decade of stagnation in the 1950s, grew by about 5 per cent per annum in the 1960s. The policy instruments of the three countries were also remarkably similar, with their emphasis on import substitution behind high protective barriers. The impact of similar policies on the patterns of growth, however, varied. Mexico performed well in both industry and agriculture as well as in exports. Pakistan did well in industry, but somewhat lagged behind in agriculture. Brazil also performed well in industry and, to a certain extent, in agriculture. While the industrialization policies of these countries had been fairly successful, excessive protection and import substitution led to the establishment of high-cost domestic industries, many of which were internationally uncompetitive.

The comparative study was the principal study of the

series, and it not only brought together the results of the industrialization policies of seven countries but, on the basis of this experience, also suggested an alternative policy package which might work more efficiently for them in the future.

It is worth mentioning here that these studies remain valuable for contemporary development economics due to their analytical approach though they were dated by the time they were completed in 1967, with most of them considering data only up to 1964–5.

◆

Among the country volumes, the study of Brazil is perhaps the most interesting to an Indian reader. Brazil is a large country—larger in area than the continental United States (US)—and it had a population of 90 million people in 1971. Its annual per capita income, at around $250 in 1971, was less than that of many of the Latin American countries, but it was above the average for the developing world. By the time of the study, Brazil had had a long experience of industrialization; in fact, by the end of the Second World War, manufacturing production had accounted for 20 per cent of the country's GDP. It had achieved remarkable progress in import substitution since the War, with manufacturing production growing at the rate of 10 per cent per annum. Unlike many developing countries, import substitution in Brazil went beyond the stage of consumer non-durables plus assembly of consumer durables, and the country also produced a wide variety of capital goods.

In addition to laying down Brazil's achievement in the area of industrialization and its policies in this context, the study also included an excellent discussion on the efficiency and cost aspects of the country's specific sectors, such as steel, automobiles, capital goods and textiles. The general conclusion drawn by the study was interesting. While many firms in Brazil were efficient producers of steel, automobiles and capital goods, the country also had many extremely inefficient textile manufacturers, the likely reason for it being that efficiency in production depended on optimum scale and modern technology, and textiles, being an old industry, did not go in for modernization since it was highly protected anyway.

The analysis of the Brazilian experience revealed several interesting points applicable for all developing countries. The first point was that economic progress often depends on the pace and extent of industrialization. A more rapid rate of industrialization itself increased capacity for economic growth by promoting the development of both the financial organization and the human resources base of the economy. Industrialization bred further industrialization; on the other hand, backwardness bred inefficiency, which made progress difficult. Perhaps this is one of the reasons why all countries have backward areas, and despite efforts, they remain backward.

The reasons for government intervention are based on dynamic considerations and involve sacrificing maximum allocative efficiency in order to shift the country to a structure of production that promotes increased income later. This is a major justification for deviation from free trade. However, indiscriminate protection over too long a period can also breed widespread inefficiency. In 1971, Brazil, like many other developing countries, had protection levels that were excessive in relation to its objectives.

Another point of interest is the importance of the scale factor in industrial efficiency. Brazil's case study brought out the fact that in many of the modern industries of the time, large firms were also the ones that were internationally competitive. For example, according to an estimate for steel plants, the economies of scale reduced the cost of production per ton of pig iron, steel ingots and flat-rolled products by 12.8, 16.5 and 28.7 per cent respectively, while output increased from 0.4 million to 1.5 million tons by 1971. Similarly, the country studies showed that insistence on domestic procurement of raw materials or parts in automobile or capital goods industries may have been pushed too far in many countries. In Brazil, the excess costs in automobile manufacturing could be cut by half if domestic procurement requirements were to be reduced to 80-5 per cent by weight from the prevailing level of about 95 per cent.

In the debate in India regarding inflation, Brazil's historical experience may be of some interest. Brazil experienced high inflation across several years—prices rose by 10 per cent a year during 1948-52, 20 per cent during 1953-60 and by as much as 90 per cent in 1964. Until 1960, however, inflation was accompanied by high growth rates, and the same policies that favoured growth also seem to have favoured inflation. There was transfer of income from wages to profits and from the private to the public sector, leading to a high level of public investment. Between 1961-70, the picture changed dramatically. Growth and industrialization lost their top priorities, public investment was reduced while current expenditure increased rapidly, and vacillating and inconsistent government policies resulted in neither stable prices nor stable growth. There was a lesson in this for India: cutting down the rate of public investment would neither help growth nor prices.

After a period of relative stagnation in the 1950s, Pakistan emerged as one of the more successful among developing countries. National income increased at around 5 per cent a year, manufacturing grew by around 15 per cent a year and exports of new manufactures registered increases of

20-5 per cent per year in the 1960s. The principal tools of economic policy in the case of Pakistan were exchange control, high protection, import licencing and export subsidies that transferred large amounts of government expenditure from the agricultural sector and urban consumers to the new industrialists. Certain inefficiencies in the allocation of resources were inevitable, but the policy, on the whole, was highly successful in achieving a high rate of manufacturing production.

It has often been argued that the tariff structure in the developing countries is such that it distorts the pattern of import substitution and leads to misallocation of resources among industries. Such misallocation does not seem to have been very significant in the case of Pakistan. The most significant determinant of the extent to which an industry produced a large proportion of the total supply domestically was the extent of its dependence on a domestically produced, rather than imported, raw material. The structure of tariff rates among industries was not a significant determinant of the structure of domestic production. For instance, the low share of domestic production in total supply of intermediates or investment and related goods was due to the lack of raw materials for most of these industries, rather than the relatively lower tariffs on competing imports.

For 30 years, from 1940 to 1970, Mexico enjoyed a sustained growth rate of 6 per cent per year. This outstanding performance was not due to industrial growth alone. Manufacturing exports increased at a rapid rate, and unlike any other developing country, agricultural production in Mexico also increased at an average rate of 4.6 per cent during the period. Inflation was modest, and Mexico was also successful in maintaining currency convertibility. As in other countries, government intervention was widespread, and the policies followed emphasized import substitution with high protection. Although Mexico was troubled by balance-of-payments difficulties from time to time, it was never pushed by these problems into adopting policies that had restrictive effects on growth.

◆

The comparative study made for depressing reading. There was plenty that seemed to have gone wrong with the industrialization strategies of the developing countries; they were richer but less equal; they were more industrialized but less efficient; they were supplying more of their own needs, but were also more dependent on imports and aid. Exports had lagged, unemployment had increased and agricultural production had suffered.

The study, at its best, analysed the ill effects of some of the industrialization policies that had been adopted. It was known that all was not well in developing countries; however, some of the quantification did come as a surprise. It was a sobering thought that a number of developing countries, including India, had established industries whose value added at world prices was negative. This meant that operating these industries required imports whose value, in foreign exchange, exceeded the price at which their output/finished product could have been imported from abroad, which meant direct losses in terms of foreign exchange and a drain on national income. A number of examples of such industries (during the early 1960s) were cited in the study: in India, leather goods, bicycles and non-ferrous metals; in Pakistan, motor vehicles, edible oils and sugar refining; in Philippines, refrigerators, air conditioners, television sets and several food products.

One can, of course, argue with some of the assumptions underlying the concept of 'value added at world prices';

for example, it is perhaps unrealistic to assume that if the domestic component manufacturers had not sold their output to, say, local automobile plants, they could have exported their output freely. However, there can be little doubt that excessive reliance on import substitution, irrespective of costs, had led to the establishment of industries whose benefits to the country were extremely small, if any.

The extent of protection against competition in many industries was also quite revealing. Very high protection in the absence of countervailing policies had certainly led to the deterioration of efficiency in many firms, as domestic profits had been guaranteed irrespective of the cost and quality of the product. A large part of growth in output—especially output per capita, which is an essential part of development—was caused by increases in technological efficiency. If protection reduced the search for better methods, better organization, better maintenance of equipment and all other elements of technological efficiency, the economy was likely to suffer a permanent and increasing cost.

On the other hand, it was also possible to argue that high effective protection may have reflected high profits (presumably taxable) rather than inefficiency in manufacturing and that protection existed for maintaining a positive balance of payments and other reasons rather than to shield uncompetitive industries. Developing countries were not alone in protecting their industries like textiles, shoes, leather and furniture. Developed countries did the same—and for the reason that they did not want competition from the developing countries! However, the basic points that emerged from the study of protection were that protection levels in the developing countries were higher than necessary to meet their objectives, and that in the absence of countervailing policies, they may have led to a bias against agriculture and exports.

If the case for specially encouraging industrialization was accepted, the authors of the comparative study readily conceded that one must also accept that there should be some bias against agriculture. However, they felt that the magnitude and effect of the bias in the countries studied had been excessive; in several of the countries, the effect on agricultural production had been damaging and agricultural exports earned less than they should have. The farmer was the main loser, having paid more for his purchases and received less for his sales than he would have if he had operated in the world market.

Due to redistribution of income from agriculture—a sector that employed the large majority of people in these countries—there had been an increase in economic inequality. Standards of living in some rural areas had started declining, although average per capita income in the country concerned may have been increasing; a particularly clear case of this is Pakistan.

Speaking of unintended effects of policy, the study included an interesting chapter on the efficiency of administrative controls. Leaving aside the intellectual bias for or against controls, many countries seemed to have been particularly inept in administering the control mechanism. There was much in the story of graft, corruption and arbitrariness of decision that gave credence to the view that in India, as in many other countries, accessibility to government officials had become a fifth factor of production! The study argued that objection to corruption was not only moral, but that corruption defeated the objectives of the discriminatory measures. In several developing countries, including India, for example, higher rates of tax were imposed on finer counts of yarn with a view to imposing higher taxes on the rich. However, tax inspectors were often bribed to classify finer counts as coarser ones, and the progressivity of the tax fell by the wayside.

Much more serious were the economic costs of delay in making decisions. Time taken to obtain various approvals from the government usually increased the marginal capital-output ratio, that is, more capital was needed to produce a given output. Manufacturers who are wise enough to anticipate delays tried to hold larger inventories of imported inputs, thereby increasing the amount of capital that needed to be invested to produce a given flow of output. If this was not done, delays led to production slowdowns and underutilization of capacity. Manufacturers, therefore, decided to play safe and pre-empt the field by applying for more imports than needed and for investment licences, even before the decision to invest had been taken.

◆

The study revealed a long catalogue of problems, which the authors believed were a direct result of government policies that had put excessive reliance on controls, administrative intervention, quantitative import restrictions and high protection. They favoured a return to a more 'open' economy and believed that developing countries would benefit from adopting a more decentralized approach with greater use of price mechanism. They were not against government intervention or special encouragement of industry, but believed that such encouragement should be in the form of 'promotional' measures rather than protective ones; for example, subsidizing the use of labour, providing training facilities and other services, improving the institutions and rewarding industry directly for any 'external' benefits which may confer.

The authors had sketched out their programme for reform in considerable detail, an outline of which is provided here. They proposed an end of quota restrictions on a permanent basis, and suggested a small uniform tariff of, say, 10 per cent on all imports, including materials and capital goods. Tariff was to have a largely non-protective role—as part of the general fiscal system, and matched by internal indirect taxes wherever possible. Although import controls could be introduced as a crisis measure, exchange rate was to be the main instrument for balance-of-payments adjustment. In countries grappling with inflation, small but very frequent adjustments of the exchange rate were considered particularly necessary.

The main encouragement to industry was to be in the form of subsidy to labour in medium- and large-scale industries, possibly at the rate of 10–50 per cent of the unskilled wage bill, depending on the country. If the government felt that there were certain industries with particularly important external economies, it might wish to give them additional special encouragement, but such cases were likely to be rare. Manufactured consumption goods were to be taxed irrespective of whether they were imported or domestically produced. Capital goods and intermediate goods were not to be taxed in the normal course. It was not that the authors believed the liberal regime could be introduced overnight; in fact, they suggested a programme for introducing the changes gradually. Initially, quotas were to be removed and the exchange rate devalued to what was considered to be the equilibrium level in the desired final solution. However, this devaluation was to be accompanied by changes in tariffs and export subsidies and taxes, so as to leave internal prices much the same as before. The transition to the final price structure was to be accomplished over a number of years by gradually reducing tariffs and export taxes and by raising indirect internal taxes while introducing subsidies.

Whether one agrees with the authors' programme for reform is largely a matter of opinion and possibly value judgment. Those who share the vision of a world with equal opportunity for all and view the problem of development as essentially one of progress along a steady growth path would find much that is attractive in this programme. On the other hand, those who consider the industrialized and the developing countries as unequal partners in trade and view the problem of development as one of structural transformation with some sacrifice of the present incomes would probably disagree.

On the basis of the evidence presented, one cannot be sure whether the policy instruments covered in the study per se were inefficient or whether the inefficiency was a result of how they were used by some countries. For example, the authors presented evidence to show that apart from Russia, the US, Spain and Portugal, protection levels in the first quarter of the twentieth century were quite low in both the developed and developing countries. However, the fact remains that while Russia and the US developed in spite of high protection, the developing countries—with low levels of protection—did not. Similarly, in terms of the effect of protection on agriculture or exports, how did the agricultural sector of Mexico and Brazil perform well despite high protection measures while that of Pakistan did not? Pakistan and Mexico experienced high growth rate of exports of manufactured goods, while Brazil did not. Levels of protection could not explain this diversity of experience. The study included a chapter which showed that many other countries, such as Taiwan, Korea and Hong Kong, had done well in exports of manufactured goods using an intelligent approach rather than by simply dismantling tariffs.

This, however, does not question the view that protection levels in many countries may have been 'excessive' and that a change in tariff structure may have been desirable. In fact, one can readily agree that rationalization of the tariff structure and reduction in average levels of protection were probably necessary in many countries for promoting efficiency.

Similarly, with regard to the effect of tariff structure on allocative efficiency, tariffs did not have a significant effect in determining the pattern of investment in Pakistan. It stands to reason that in countries that have a licencing policy for investment, tariffs are unlikely to be the primary influence on pattern of investment, since private investment is hardly free to move in response to differential profitability in different lines. Since the average protection was high, it was likely that tariffs affected the pace rather than the direction of investment. Again, one does not wish to suggest that the licencing policy had achieved its objectives and the allocation of resources had been optimal; only that if this was not so, it was not necessarily because of tariffs.

The authors were right in suggesting that the move to import-substitution policies in the developing countries had been due to export pessimism and that the accent on import substitution had not decreased any country's dependence on imports. While it was true that, in absolute terms, imports had not decreased, there was no clear evidence about whether it held true relative to the rate of industrial growth that was achieved. The development strategy of countries had depended on the view they had taken of opportunities in international trade, and some of the countries may have been too pessimistic. However, it was true that for the developing world as a whole, in spite of extraordinary growth in their manufactured exports, of about 13 per cent per year between 1959 and 1966, their total exports (including oil countries) increased at about 6 per cent. The share of developing countries in world trade declined from 27 per cent in 1953 to 19 per cent in 1967; even in primary products, their share had fallen from 54 per cent to 42 per cent. For the developing countries as a group, this was hardly conducive to optimism.

It is possible to argue that the developing countries would have done better if they had pursued more outward-looking policies; but the question remains: how much better? Manufactured goods were still a minor fraction of total exports, and even if they grew at the rate of 15–20 per cent, they couldn't have made up for the stagnation in exports of traditional items such as foodstuffs and agricultural raw materials. The only likely strategy for some countries was to accelerate the pace of industrialization, while relatively decreasing their dependence on imports.

How opportunities in trade are perceived and evaluated tends to vary from country to country, and so does the 'openness' of their economies. It is also possible that the degree to which a country wants to participate in international trade is not entirely a matter of current economic costs and benefits. Some countries, which are too dependent on economic developments abroad or which rely on exports of one or two commodities for a large part of their national income, might be willing to pay a price (in terms of a lower current income) in order to reduce their dependence. Others might want to decrease their dependence on certain types of goods, or on certain countries, and pay a certain price for it. Self-sufficiency in food production, for example, is an objective that seems to command universal approval. It does not seem possible to recommend a desirable degree of 'openness' for all developing countries without introducing a prior value judgment.

It is likely that a policy of periodic exchange rate adjustments would avoid balance-of-payments problems, but the interesting question is: at what level of income growth? For many countries, a sound balance of payments is the easiest thing to achieve—they only have to stop growing!

The suggestion that the developing countries should devalue the rate of exchange and then gradually adjust tariffs and subsidies is somewhat wishful. It is difficult to find an equilibrium rate of exchange that is valid at a point of time, let alone one that is fixed through time. If the developing countries were to adopt this policy, they were likely to find themselves pursuing a shifting goal—and continuously devaluing.

Taken as a whole, the programme for reform suggested in the study was not convincing. The individual policies recommended may have been valid to varying degrees in different countries—for example, there may have been a case for labour subsidies or for exchange rate adjustment or rationalization of the tariff structure—but the past experience with industrialization policies presented in the studies did not necessarily point to an abandonment of the development strategies that the developing countries had pursued so far.

If the programme was not convincing, what else could be done? It is obvious that there were no easy—or even difficult— universal answers to the problems of industrialization. It is also likely that irrespective of a different approach being followed, the course of development would have never run smooth. However, some elements of a more rational industrial policy—one which is neutral with respect to value judgments or political systems—may be suggested.

First, there is the need for consistency in decision-making when planning for development. The impact of development activities or policies should be judged as a whole rather than piecemeal in terms of the effect of each individual policy or activity. One policy may be justified because it promotes equality, another because it creates employment or investment or exports or import substitution; yet taken together, the programme may help neither equality nor growth nor economic independence. Individual decisions are necessarily made at various levels and in various departments, and in order for these to be mutually consistent, it is essential that development objectives are articulated more specifically than, say, the desire for 'full employment' or 'social equality' or 'import substitution'. For example, an employment-oriented programme does not necessarily mean that a country will adopt any project that can employ more people; it may only mean that such projects will be given some preference over others. How much preference and at what cost to other objectives—these are not matters of technical analysis but of political judgment, which only the country's leadership can decide.

Second, it needs to be recognized that whatever one wishes to do, one should try to ensure that expected benefits are larger than costs. For this, it is essential to do a social cost-benefit analysis of industrial activities. Developing countries generally tend to neglect this aspect and this lacuna in project selection, rather than levels of protection, can probably explain why many food projects are technically and economically inefficient. No amount of nationalism or inward-looking strategy can justify an industrial project that consumes more in real terms than it produces; yet, many countries have at least a few projects that are precisely of this nature. It must be emphasized that social cost-benefit analysis of projects has nothing to do with the controversy over public vs private sector or controls or the extent of planning. All economic activities yield certain costs and benefits to society, and it is essential to quantify their social value in order to determine whether the costs are worth the benefits.

Third, whatever views one might have on the allocative efficiency of price mechanism or controls, productive efficiency in the use of resources is a must. Once the decision to produce a commodity has been taken, it does not make sense to use more resources than required to produce a unit of output, unless one can justify the additional cost in terms of a more than corresponding gain in some other objective. For example, some countries encourage—and sometimes even insist on—the establishment of numerous production units even in cases where, for the given market size, one plant is sufficient and a better option in terms of realizing economies of scale and lower costs. A number of plants, each below optimum capacity, may be vaguely justified in terms of some other objective, such as regional equality or dispersal of ownership. However, on closer examination, it may be found that the other benefits are largely imaginary, since all the plants are located in the more advanced regions and owned by the same group of industrialists, or that the excess cost of sub-optimum plants far outweigh the social gain.

Finally, rationalization need not necessarily mean a decrease in the average level of government or public control of economic activities; it means that the system of controls should be internally consistent and that individual controls should produce demonstrable benefits in terms of the country's objectives. Administrative ability, no less than material resources, is scarce in developing countries, and it is necessary that it be efficiently allocated. There is really no point in continuing with controls that, however regrettably, cannot be administered.

These suggestions add up to a plea for rationality and cost-consciousness in the pursuit of development objectives and, if adopted, are likely to avoid many of the inefficiencies in resource utilization that many developing countries, including India, have adopted to accelerate the process of industrialization.

2

THE QUEST FOR SELF-RELIANCE

In the 1960s, all the developing countries were planning for self-sustaining growth such that they could generate acceptable rates of investment and growth out of their own resources. Such 'ultimate' self-reliance was the explicit objective of all normal planning exercises and development strategies of the time. There may have been situations when a country, either as a result of realistic assessment of aid possibilities in the future or as a matter of internal or external political objective, may have decided to terminate aid before the point of self-sustaining growth was reached and well ahead of the anticipations of its own perspective plans. This required a mid-course adjustment in the direction of the economy and adoption of policies specifically directed towards a reduction in the country's external dependence in the short- or medium-term.

SPECIFICATION OF THE OBJECTIVE

The word 'self-reliance' can mean different things to different people, and the first need is to define it in more concrete and quantifiable terms as a statement of a country's objective. Thus, in one sense, 'self-reliance' may refer to the objective of national or intra-national self-sufficiency or the minimization of the country's external or internal trade. This is the sense in which the word is used when one speaks of communities that grow their own vegetables and meet basic needs as being self-reliant or of import substitution as a step towards self-reliance. National self-sufficiency in food and certain other basic commodities (for example, steel and fertilizers) is thus frequently considered as being synonymous with self-reliance.

In another sense, self-reliance may refer to the elimination of aid—either gross or net. Elimination of gross aid at some future date is implicit in the objective of 'self-sustaining growth' espoused by all developing countries. It is also implicit in the international consensus on the desirability of relating the terms of assistance to the debt-servicing capacity of the developing countries. For countries which have been borrowing for a long time, the distinction between gross and net can be quantitatively very significant. However, a formulation of self-reliance targets in terms of net aid is odd and perplexing. Since aid negotiations and decisions are almost always made in terms of gross aid, it may lead to the paradoxical situation where the country becomes technically 'self-reliant', but its quest for fresh aid intensifies! This could happen when fresh inflows of aid are falling over time while debt service obligations are increasing. Sometime in the future, the two would become equal, and the country would actually have to seek greater fresh aid from that point onwards in order to meet its rising debt service obligations. Otherwise, the country would soon become 'over self-reliant'. This is a somewhat unwieldy concept and can be easily avoided by defining self-reliance as the state when gross aid is zero, and choosing an appropriate time horizon for achieving this.

Choice of an appropriate time horizon is crucial for giving operational meaning to the objective of self-reliance. Aid that is not stolen is either consumed or invested in new projects or used for sustaining the existing industrial structure. Ceteris paribus, elimination of aid is, therefore, likely to affect the growth rate of income or investment or both, and there is likely to be a clear trade-off between the growth rate and investment on the one hand and the level and duration of aid on the other. Much as one may want to have self-reliance as soon as possible, the question of an appropriate time horizon requires a little more than finding out the terminal date of the nearest plan. Such a choice can be made only after an assessment of the trade-offs between investment/growth and self-reliance at different points of time.

However, there may be situations when no such choice with respect to time horizon exists—either because of internal political reasons or because of decisions made by others over which the country has no control. In such cases, the only important question is the period of time over which the country's balance of payments has to adjust itself to the new situation. Due to the availability of short-term balance-of-payments support—primarily from the IMF—and reserves, the period over which such adjustment is to be achieved may be longer than the date at which aid is to be terminated. Depending on the magnitude and complexity of the adjustment problem, a country may, therefore, choose to run deficit in its balance of payments beyond the date of aid termination and finance it out of short-term borrowings or reserves. This is tantamount to 'stretching' the time horizon for effective self-reliance.

Whatever the time horizon, it is clear that self-reliance would be the easiest thing to achieve if there were no other growth or development objectives that had to be satisfied at the same time. All countries, developed and developing, have a multiplicity of objectives, and the decision to eliminate aid may affect any one or more of them. In considering a policy frame for self-reliance, it is, therefore, necessary to specify the minimum of other aid-dependent objectives that have to be met at the same time. For example, a country may have been receiving aid for increase in 'essential' consumption (for example, food imports), growth in industrial production (for example, raw material imports) and new investment (for example, capital goods). Elimination of aid may affect the target growth rate in all these areas, and in planning for self-reliance, it may become necessary to consider the trade-offs, if any, among these different objectives (for example, new investment vs capacity utilization in existing industries). In some dependent economies, the sum of minimum expectations in all areas may turn out to be inconsistent with self-reliance over the chosen time horizon. In such cases, either expectations in some areas have to be reduced or the time horizon needs to be stretched.

POLICY INSTRUMENTS

Self-reliance over a given period would require adoption of a policy framework calculated to increase the savings rate (over what it would have been if aid was taken) as well as an improvement in the balance of payments. In some cases, the two processes would mean much the same thing; for example, when export surpluses provide the bulk of investible resources or when savings are sought to be increased by reduction in consumer imports. In some cases, however, separate policies for savings and balance of payments may be required; for example, when a balance-of-payments deficit is sought to be met through a reduction in imports of investment goods.

There are three further points which need to be emphasized before a discussion of specific policies: (i) for the purpose of this discussion, we will focus only on policies that would bring forth the additional effort required for self-reliance, over and above what the country would have done otherwise;

(ii) policies that have a recognizable pay-off in the short and medium term are ipso facto superior to those with uncertain pay-off in the future. This is so because an unexpected balance-of-payments crisis (and the consequent 'bailing out' operation by creditors) in the course of vigorous pursuit of self-reliance may be avoided by developed countries and (iii) the discussion limits itself to feasible policy alternatives in real economies and does not deal with 'optimal' policies in idealized economies which satisfy the conditions necessary for general equilibrium. Pretence of technical objectivity notwithstanding, much of the economic discussion of public issues (especially when the countries concerned are 'somewhere out there' rather than one's own) suffers from a value bias in favour of policies that promote a preferred economic system or a preferred form of economic organization. The following discussion attempts to steer clear of presumptions regarding superiority of one sort of measures over others on value grounds, although it must be recognized that a country could quite legitimately choose to reject some of the available options on precisely these grounds.

The habitual response of governments seized by a desire for self-reliance is to wish for faster growth in exports and import substitution. While one can have little against these policies as such, the trouble with both these courses of action is that their outcome is often likely to be outside the control of the authorities. The issue here is not whether exports can grow or whether the pace of import substitution can be strengthened, but if they can be made to grow faster than the growth rates forecasted prior to the adoption of the self-reliance objective. In some countries, it may be possible to do so, but in others, it may not be. It would depend on: (i) how optimistic the export and import projections were to begin with and (ii) the length of the time horizon chosen for self-reliance. The more ambitious the original targets and the shorter the time horizon, the greater is the likelihood of exclusive reliance on these policies not being feasible. Therefore, unless one can demonstrate precisely how a faster growth rate of exports or import substitution is to be brought about, self-reliance through these policies cannot be considered a credible objective.

It has sometimes been suggested that exports can be increased at any rate, provided a country is willing to follow a policy of a 'realistic' or 'equilibrium' exchange rate. However, not only is the concept of equilibrium rate in a growing and changing economy of doubtful theoretical validity, there are also other considerations that severely restrict the utility of this suggestion. Such a policy cannot be pursued by all developing countries at the same time, since a large part of their exports are non-competitive with those of the industrialized countries and face a low elasticity of demand. For any particular country, on the other hand, exports at any price that the foreigners are willing to pay is a feasible option only if exports play an extremely marginal role in the economy. Otherwise, loss in welfare and income through deterioration in terms of trade would become significant and self-defeating.

The possibility of import substitution depends upon: (i) the composition of existing imports; (ii) the stage of development of the economy and (iii) the import intensity of domestic production. In all aid-dependent economies, import intensity of domestic production outside of agriculture and simple resource-based manufacturing is likely to be high in terms of both raw material inputs and the initial capital investment. This becomes a matter of crucial importance if the structure of current imports is such that further substitution can be attempted only in industries with a long gestation period. During the initial period, absolute dependence on imports in such cases is likely to increase rather than decrease. Paradoxically, therefore, accelerated import substitution for self-reliance in the short- or medium-term may be feasible only in countries that are either too underdeveloped (and, therefore, provide scope for import substitution in simple lines) or highly developed, with a well-diversified economic structure.

In countries where additional exports or additional import-substitution do not provide feasible routes to self-reliance, other policies for achieving a turnaround in balance of payments have to be considered. These are likely to consist of the following: (i) change in industrial priorities in order to reduce import dependence per unit of investment/output; (ii) cut in imports (as distinguished from import substitution) within the pattern of investment and (iii) rescheduling of debt service obligation on past loans.

It may be recalled that developing countries faced with a 'foreign exchange constraint' are frequently urged to go for the first option. The desirability of this policy under any given circumstances should, however, depend on whether the change in priorities can be accomplished within the framework of a country's chosen development strategy and is in keeping with its long-term development objective, or whether it calls for a major departure from the chosen strategy. When it is the latter—for example, when a shift away from heavy industries to light industries or from industry to agriculture is involved—this course of action would affect not only the pace of development but also its content. This is tantamount to salvaging the present by mortgaging the future and must, therefore, be resisted.

A planned cut in imports, painful as it is, is one of the most effective courses of action in the short- and medium-term—and indeed what most countries do in the event of a balance-of-payments crisis. In a crisis, however, the measure becomes unnecessarily disruptive of development since imports are cut either across the board or on an item-by-item basis without sufficient regard for inter-industry relations and small economic costs. In the absence of aid, the level of imports needs to be reduced. It is much better to do so over a period of time and on the basis of economic criteria that are likely to maximize the development impact of any planned level of imports. Opinions, of course, vary on what constitutes 'development impact', and each country will have to decide this for itself. For countries where imports are already down to the bone, the choice will be particularly difficult: they may well have to choose between the claim of existing industries and the need for new investment in the long-run development of the economy.

Rescheduling of debt service obligations on past development loans can be an eminently sensible course of action for countries opting for premature self-reliance, especially when outstanding debt is high. However, rescheduling can take various forms, and some of them can do more harm than good. It is, therefore, necessary to lay down the conditions for a successful arrangement: (i) rescheduling should cover all development loans. Partial rescheduling, according to either source or terms of loans, is likely to create more burden-sharing problems among aid-giving countries than it solves; (ii) rescheduling should cover as long a period as possible and (iii) the rescheduled amount should bear near-zero interest.

The success of rescheduling operations depends on the attitude of the creditors. In the past, their attitude has not been overly helpful and rescheduling has taken the form of short-term bailing out operations in response to debt crises (except in the case of India) and has usually carried stiff terms and conditions with it. In part, this attitude has been conditioned by the fact that many of these crises had arisen because of gross mismanagement of the economy by present or past governments.

Proposals for rescheduling in the context of self-reliance, however, have to be sharply distinguished from such past cases. The presumption of bad management should not normally arise and since the total commitment of the aid-givers would be decreasing in the future, it may be assumed that their desire to keep the receiving country on a short leash would also be less. There would certainly be a minor income loss to the aid-givers as a result of rescheduling, but this would be more than compensated by gain from stoppage of aid. However, if pursuant to political reasons (or prejudice) aid-givers are still reluctant, unilateral action by the borrower cannot be ruled out.

To sum up, it is clear that the set of policies necessary for self-reliance is likely to vary from one country to another, depending on factors such as the chosen development strategy, the present stage of development, the time horizon, the composition of its imports, and so on. In some cases, the choice of policies would be fairly easy; in others, painful choices would have to be made between conflicting ends. In most cases, however, if the desire for self-reliance is to become a credible objective of development policy, it is likely that much more would be needed than just exhortation for more exports or import substitution.

THE INDIAN CASE

More than most other developing countries, India tried to relate its policy framework to the long-term perspective of development. Undaunted by external circumstances and temporary setbacks, in each successive plan, allocation and priority decisions had thus broadly been in conformity with the long-term strategy, which was identified soon after Independence. Programming of foreign aid, however, had been an important exception. There had been no clear strategy and the Indian attitude to aid and self-reliance has fluctuated sharply from one year to the next, depending on requirements and other circumstances.

During the First Five-Year Plan, the attitude to aid was conditioned by three factors: (i) India had large sterling reserves which, together with exports, could be expected to cover the external requirements of the Plan; (ii) Soviet Russia had planned 'successfully' without relying on outside assistance and (iii) India had wanted to play an active and, possibly, a balancing role in foreign affairs. It, therefore, could not risk outside interference. Accordingly, the First Plan was firmly (and loudly) self-reliant, and allowed for only a minimal role for foreign aid in India's development. It laid down that 'external assistance is acceptable only if it carries with it no conditions, explicit or implicit, which affect even remotely the country's ability to take an independent line in international affairs'. During this period, India asked for and received very little aid (amounting to ₹204 crore).

The declining sterling reserves, the much larger resource requirements of the Second Plan and finally the balance-of-payments crisis of 1958, however, soon transformed this attitude. During the crisis (India had lost ₹500 crore in reserves in the first two years of the Second Plan), the Aid India Consortium was organized and a complete disruption of the country's external finances was successfully prevented. This experience had a profound effect on the planners, and India became firmly pro-aid. It had planned for about ₹800 crore by way of aid during the Second Plan, but ended up using

₹1,500 crore (21 per cent of the Plan investment).

The fondness for aid was fully reflected in the financial arrangements, as the Third Plan provided for (and received) ₹2,200 crore by way of aid (36 per cent of the Plan investment). Reliance on large inflow of aid was explained thus: 'it would be advantageous from the point of view of recipient countries as well as donors to plan for substantial amounts of external assistance for relatively short period rather than proceed with varying and uncertain amounts over an indefinite period.' The period of the Third Plan, however, coincided with the period of 'aid-weariness' in donor countries and mounting tensions in the aid relationship resulting from excessive interference by aid agencies in economic policies of the recipient countries. The latter years of the Plan, which culminated in the devaluation of the rupee, and the subsequent three years of Annual Plans were particularly difficult for India economically, and marked the beginning of the era of disillusionment and discontent with regard to aid.

The Fourth Plan was formulated during the period when foreign aid to India had begun to decline and debt service payments were increasing sharply. There was also considerable international pessimism about the future of aid. These factors shaped the Plan strategy with regard to aid, and for the first time, a specific date was laid down for the elimination of aid. Aid, net of debt service payments, was to be reduced to half the 'current level' by the end of the Fourth Plan (1980–1). Interestingly enough, the Fourth Plan objective was fulfilled in 1971–2, and net aid was less than half the average net receipts during the Third Plan or the three Annual Plans.

Insofar as this can be termed self-reliance, it was entirely the result of decisions made outside the country, and was accompanied not by an increase but by a substantial shortfall in the rate of savings. Balance of payments was held in check not by exports shooting up to meet the rising import requirements of a high-growth economy, but by a substantial decline in imports consequent upon a fall in the rate of investment and industrial production.

The emphasis on self-reliance has to be considered against this background. It is clear that self-reliance alone is not enough; in order for it to be meaningful, it has to be accompanied by an acceptable measure of progress towards other development objectives. An important task, therefore, is to redefine self-reliance and other development objectives in a way that would be operational as well as mutually consistent.

3

TO TAX OR NOT TO TAX

It is generally agreed that the guiding principle behind corporate taxation in a developing country like India should be to raise maximum revenue from the corporate sector. This is, of course, subject to the constraint that the rate and structure of taxation should be such as to permit and persuade the corporate sector to fulfil the economic role assigned to it. It is also generally agreed that the objectives vis-à-vis the corporate sector, in the promotion of which fiscal policy might play a part, are as follows:

(i) Corporate sector should be encouraged to produce and sell more by fully utilizing the existing capacities, particularly in 'priority' areas. Similarly, the total quantum of investment should increase at a high rate;
(ii) There should be wider diffusion of ownership and less concentration in the growth of investment;
(iii) There should be wider geographical diffusion of new investment, particularly in the backward areas and
(iv) In the choice of markets for its products and choice of technology, the corporate sector should be encouraged to place more emphasis on exports and employment.

There are a number of other minor objectives, but the ones listed above are the most important and to respond to which the system of corporate taxation was designed in the 1970s in particular. Keeping these in mind, let us examine some specific issues relating to corporate taxation under the following three heads: (i) the base of taxation; (ii) the rate of taxation and (iii) tax incentives for promotion of desired goals. It should be mentioned that in considering these issues, an important objective is to analyse the impact and incidence of taxation on the behaviour of the private corporate sector. So far as the public-sector corporations are concerned, it can be assumed that the rate and structure of taxation is not an important influence in determining their operations.

THE BASE OF TAXATION

Here, the most important issue is whether the base of taxation should be income or wealth or both. At present, income (or, more correctly, profits) serves as the base, but it is being questioned whether corporations should be taxed on the use of capital resources instead, irrespective of whether they make profits on the use of such resources. In fact, it has been argued that there is all the more reason for taxing a company which uses capital but does not do so 'productively'. Another reason for this view is that interest payments are deductible for tax purposes, and thus the system favours borrowed capital, most of which is supplied by public-sector institutions and banks.

The idea of a capital tax ipso facto is attractive in a capital-scarce country, particularly one which is also searching for fresh avenues for raising tax resources. Similarly, the fact that the present system of taxation is biased in favour of borrowed capital is also true. The logic of excluding interest for tax purposes is that interest is like any other item of cost to the borrowing firm. While there is some force in this logic, the problem still remains that under the present system of taxation, it is much cheaper for a firm to borrow funds than to raise capital in the form of equity.

Given this bias, the question that arises is whether it is desirable to remove this bias through fiscal action. The answer would seem to be in the affirmative. Even among the profitable firms today, there is a tendency to distribute their profits in the form of high dividends or accumulate reserves rather than reduce their borrowings. Since most borrowing institutions are publicly owned, it may be argued that the shyness on the part of many financially strong firms to raise their capital requirements in the market adversely affects the total mobilization of savings in the economy.

If a strong case can be made for making borrowed capital more expensive and for removing, at least to a certain extent, the existing bias in favour of borrowed capital, some alternative policy instruments that could accomplish both objectives may be considered. There are three possibilities: (i) increase in the interest rate; (ii) tax on capital employed and (iii) tax on interest payments alone. All these measures are designed to raise the cost of capital. While an increase in the interest rate would raise the cost of capital investment, paradoxical as it may seem, it will not necessarily remove the bias in favour of borrowed capital. This is because if the cost of borrowing is raised, it would also raise the minimum rate of profit that is acceptable to the investor. The relative tax advantage of borrowing as against raising equity capital for financing a given volume of investment would, therefore, still remain.

A small tax on the stock of capital as well as on the flow of interest payments is feasible. Either of these taxes can be designed to accomplish both the objectives mentioned earlier. A tax on capital employed can be at a differentiated rate with a stiffer rate of tax on borrowed capital. Similarly, a tax on interest payments would raise the cost of borrowed capital to the firm beyond what it would be at any given level of interest rate and thus somewhat reduce the bias in favour of excessive capitalization based on borrowed funds. One disadvantage of the tax on interest payments is that for existing firms that are not growth-oriented, it may not provide an incentive for more efficient use of the existing capital. Therefore, subject to administrative convenience, it is to be considered whether a tax on capital employed (differentiated according to borrowed or owned capital) may not be preferable.

If such a tax is introduced, it would need to be considered whether the nominal rate of tax on profit should be somewhat reduced. An argument against this course of action is that a reduction in the nominal rate of tax on profits might reduce the incentive for more efficient use of capital in the existing firms, since firms are already used to the present rate of taxation. A more powerful argument is that any reduction in the existing rate of tax on profits may confer unintended benefits to those companies which, by the nature of their operations, use lower capital, trading companies being one such example. On balance, it seems that a tax on capital employed should be thought of as an additional tax, and would, therefore, have to be of a small magnitude.

THE RATE OF TAXATION

The primary issues regarding the rate of taxation are: (i) what should be the rate of taxation? (ii) should the taxation rates be progressive depending on income or capacity to pay? (iii) should these rates vary for different firms depending on the structure of ownership (for example, closely held vs widely held), profit-distribution policies or the source of corporate income (for example, income from inter-corporate investment)? It may be mentioned that there is a surcharge in addition to the basic rate of corporate tax. The surcharge has the same effect as raising the basic rate by a certain percentage, and there is no reason why it should not be merged with the basic rate. However, if it is necessary to have a separate surcharge for cosmetic reasons, there should be no objection to it on economic grounds.

Regarding the rate of taxation, it should be mentioned that although the nominal rates in the early 1970s were 55 per cent or more (except in case of a widely held domestic company with income of less than ₹1 lakh, where the rate was 45 per cent), the effective rate of tax varied a great deal among different firms and industries. For 1,229 out of 1,650 profit-making companies, tax as a proportion of profit was around 42 per cent in 1971–2; for several industry groups, the percentage was much lower; for example, shipping (7.2 per cent), aluminium (13.7 per cent), paper (23.7 per cent) and cement (33.6 per cent). The difference between effective and nominal rates arises because of the operation of various fiscal incentives (most important of which is development rebate), and in so far as the concessions can be assumed to have promoted desired objectives, there is nothing particularly objectionable about this. The relevant question in judging whether present tax rates are too high (or too low) is whether at these rates, firms can make reasonable profits on their net worth or on paid-up capital. While whether a particular rate of profit can be considered to be adequate or reasonable depends on the opportunity cost of capital, risk and the role assigned to the corporate sector, the answer to this question, largely, seems to be yes. In 1971–2, for profit-making companies, after-tax profit as percentage of net worth was 12.9 per cent and after-tax profit (minus preference dividend) as percentage or ordinary paid-up capital was 26.6 per cent. These rates of after-tax profit seemed adequate, and it seems that the effective rates of corporate tax in that period cannot be considered too high. Such indications as are available from partial data for the early 1970s do not show that there was a net deterioration in profitability of the corporate sector or that firms were driven out of business because of abolition of development rebate. The adequacy of profit rate would, however, need to be reviewed from time to time in view of the changes in tax structure.

As regards the question about whether or not taxation rates should be progressive, a certain degree of progression according to income is built into the tax structure whereby widely held domestic companies pay a lower rate of tax (45 per cent) on incomes below ₹1 lakh and closely held companies pay a lower rate of tax (55 per cent) on incomes below ₹2 lakh. Before discussing the rationale for this distinction, an important question to consider is whether rates should be progressive in principle.

The case for progression is based on the capacity to pay as well as on the objective of actively discouraging large companies which presumably have larger absolute incomes. However, the case against such a course is more persuasive. Firstly, income is related to assets, and in many areas, technology requires larger capital base and hence, the firm must generate larger absolute incomes. Secondly, progressive rates would encourage floating of new companies for each part of the manufacturing process and may, therefore, be wasteful of capital use. Lastly, it would act as a major disincentive for capacity expansion and realization of the economies of scale.

On balance, it seems that the introduction of progression in rates of corporate tax similar to personal income tax slabs would be undesirable. However, the proposition of smaller firms being more favourably treated needs to be examined. It may be argued that smaller and newer firms face great difficulty in raising capital and, therefore, have to rely on generating funds internally for further growth. The fact, however, remains that the tax concessions apply only to incomes below a certain level and so, they do not always accrue to the small-scale sector. It needs to be considered whether the size of the firm would be a more appropriate criterion for concessional treatment. Doing so would discourage firms from taking advantage of economies of scale and expanding beyond the size where tax concession would not be available. This fragmentation of firms may lead to wasteful use of capital. The balance of advantages in the concessional treatment of firms (by size vs by income) is thus not clear, and it needs to be considered whether simple rules for such a tax concession may be devised which would meet the desired objective without undue sacrifice of revenue or efficiency.

As regards the question of whether tax rates should vary for different firms, the taxation rate differs between firms depending on: (i) whether the firm is closely held or widely held; (ii) whether it is a domestic company or a foreign company; (iii) in case of a closely held company, whether it distributes a certain percentage of its profits and (iv) the proportion of its income that is derived from inter-corporate investment.

The rationale for levying a higher rate of tax on closely held companies is to discourage high-income groups from forming such companies for tax avoidance. The force of the argument has, of course, considerably diminished in view of the reduction in marginal rates of taxes on personal income. Another factor that poses a difficulty in having different rates of taxation is the administrative problem in distinguishing between a closely held and a widely held company. While there was once a good economic case for abolishing the distinction, one argument in favour of retaining it at that point in time was that such discrimination persuaded companies to go public, which rendered them subject to the discipline of public scrutiny.

Differential tax rates for foreign and domestic companies were desirable in view of the existing policy towards foreign investment and dilution of equity. Apart from the question of policy towards foreign investment, this distinction was believed to be important for administrative reasons also. It is difficult to realize personal taxes from recipients of the distributed profits of foreign companies, and a higher rate of company taxation is, therefore, believed to be the only method of compounding the tax, which would otherwise have been paid by the recipients of distributed profits.

The attitude of the tax system towards distribution of profits was somewhat ambivalent. In case of widely held public companies, there was an incentive to retain profits since distributed profits are taxed in the hands of shareholders and are thus subject to double taxation. In the case of closely held companies, the position was the other way round. They are required to distribute their profits up to a prescribed percentage of their distributable income, failing which they are liable to pay an additional amount of income tax calculated on their undistributed profits.

The most persuasive argument in favour of distribution of profits was that it makes allocation of savings subject to public control. At the same time, a reasonable argument against such a distribution is the savings argument, and the need to provide owned resources for growth and expansion. The compulsion for growth is likely to be greater when internally generated resources are available for financing. Perhaps the pros and cons more or less even out and, on balance, it seems that in principle the fiscal system should be neutral as between distribution and retention of profits.

Although it has been argued that double taxation of dividends introduces a bias in favour of retention of profits, it is difficult to substantiate this with any empirical evidence. In so far as the rate of dividend declared is taken as an indicator of the financial soundness of the firm for purposes of raising capital and also has an influence on the price of shares, there is already a certain amount of pressure on the firms to declare dividends at the rates that are prevalent in the market, and one cannot be sure whether further exemption would necessarily increase the rate of distribution. The choice between retention and distribution of profits is more likely to be influenced by the investment plans of the firms rather than by the rate of personal taxation on dividends.

The present provision regarding compulsory declaration of dividends in the case of closely held companies is believed to be administratively cumbersome as well as ineffective because of a large number of exemptions that are granted from this provision to industrial and other type of companies from time to time. The Taxation Laws (Amendment) Bill, 1973, withdrew some of these exemptions, namely those available to industrial companies and companies having capital investment of ₹50 lakh or more, while at the same time reducing the statutory percentage of compulsory distribution in the case of such companies to 45 per cent. In the case of closely held companies, compulsory distribution was useful to render the allocation of such savings subject to public scrutiny as well as to prevent avoidance of tax. Since in any case, for purposes of determining the rate of taxation, the distinction between closely held and widely held companies is maintained, the provision regarding compulsory distribution need not cause any further administrative complication. It is, however, desirable to narrow the list of exemptions for this purpose as well as to diminish the area of administrative discretion in determining whether a company is subject to the provision of compulsory distribution or not.

Finally, there is the question of taxation of inter-corporate dividends. Inter-corporate dividends bear a reduced rate of corporation tax. In computing the total income of the company, a specified percentage of dividend income received by it from another company is allowed as a straight deduction. The effective rate of taxation for domestic companies varies from about 28 per cent to 41 per cent, depending upon the rate of corporation tax applicable to the company. In order to put the problem of inter-corporate investment in perspective, it should also be mentioned that at present, inter-corporate investment is subject to a number of restrictions under the Companies Act. A company can invest a maximum of 30 per cent of its subscribed capital in other companies (and only 20 per cent within the same 'group'). Further, investment in any individual company should not exceed more than 10 per cent of the subscribed capital of the latter.

In view of the need for further investment in many areas where critical shortages are acting as impediments for industrial development of the country, it is worth examining whether our policies for inter-corporate investment can be altered to conform to the needs of the present economic situation. To the extent that companies have investible resources which they cannot or do not wish to use for further expansion in their own line of activity, a strong case can be made for providing an incentive for investment of these resources in critical sectors, such as cement, fertilizer, power, paper, and so on. On any rational economic criteria, the social benefits of additional production in these areas are likely to far outweigh any social costs arising from accelerated inter-corporate investment activity. If so, an alternative to the present policy may be to permit inter-corporate investment in industries in the core sector without restriction and subject them to concessional rates of taxation which, if necessary, may be even lower than the present rate. For investment in non-priority areas, on the other hand, the present tax concession can be withdrawn, and investment in this area may continue to be subject to present limits on investment by one company into the equity of another. This package is unlikely to involve the government in a revenue loss, and to the extent that inter-corporate investment would have greater incentive to go into priority areas, it would certainly be preferable to the present system.

TAX INCENTIVES

There is also a system of tax incentives, which is fairly comprehensive and covers a host of desirable objectives. Thus, for new investment, there is a five-year 'tax holiday' and the initial depreciation allowance, which replaces the development rebate. Investment subsidy as well as other tax incentives are provided for setting up industries in backward areas. Incentives are also available for transmission of technical know-how, shifting of industrial undertakings from congested urban areas, research and development (R&D), promoting export markets, and so on.

This list of incentives perhaps needs to be rationalized. In a system where a tax incentive is available for everything that may be considered even remotely worthwhile, the efficacy of fiscal incentives in promoting an individual objective becomes that much less since an alternative is always available to a firm. However, in view of the strong case that can be made for each of the existing incentives, taken individually and in isolation from the entire system of incentives, it must be recognized that it will not be possible to eliminate any of these incentives. The only question, therefore, is whether the present set of incentives should be further augmented to promote other worthwhile objectives.

There are three objectives that may be considered for further tax concessions: (i) the need to encourage more investment in priority industries; (ii) promotion of exports and (iii) more employment. So far as more investment is concerned, it is true that initial depreciation allowance has now been introduced. However, it is believed that this concession does not really mitigate problems of some highly capital-intensive industries which are price-controlled and where prices cannot be revised adequately because of one reason or another. If this is true, there is a case for a flexible fiscal policy that provides further tax concessions. For a restricted group of high-priority price-controlled industries where prices cannot be adequately revised to take into consideration the full extent of increase in costs, the issue under consideration is the way in which fiscal relief should be granted. Other possibilities are: (i) a straight tax relief of a certain percentage on profits; (ii) free depreciation and (iii) development rebate so that, in effect, the deductible depreciation is more than 100 per cent of the capital investment. Depending on the extent of the relief that is needed, alternatives (ii) and (iii) would seem to be preferable to (i), as the incidence of benefit would vary according to investment rather than the level of profits.

For encouraging exports, it may be desirable to tax all income from exports at a lower rate. Such a scheme has also been tried in the past. The main problem is that its benefit does not relate to additional exports and as such the revenue cost of such a scheme may be completely out of proportion to the benefit. It also seems that a scheme that subsidizes exports over the whole range is an alternative to a change in the exchange rate rather than an incentive for exports at the margin.

As mentioned earlier, the effective rate of taxation on a

number of firms and industries is actually low, and in many cases, considerably below the average. This is, of course, due to the operation of development rebate and other incentives. It needs to be considered whether a minimum rate of corporate tax of, say, 15 per cent out of profits (after costs) can be introduced for all firms.

4

SAVED BY NRIS

Transfer of savings by NRIs can take the form of: (i) remittance for consumption or investment that cannot be repatriated; (ii) savings deposits with Indian banks or other investments that are liable to be repatriated in the future and (iii) imports of goods (for example, machinery). Although transfer of savings in any of these forms adds to foreign exchange resources of the country, the net balance-of-payments impact of each of these alternatives is different. Remittances add to the country's foreign exchange reserves and are available to the government for expenditure. The net balance-of-payments gain, therefore, is 100 per cent of the amount of remittance. Deposits, on the other hand, are analogous to commercial borrowings abroad since the initial inflow of funds would be partially or wholly offset by repatriation in subsequent years. However, to the extent that a part of these savings ultimately remain at home, there is a positive gain to the balance of payments (as compared to commercial borrowings). So far as special facilities for import of machinery are concerned, they improve the balance of payments only to the extent that machineries thus imported are essential and would have been imported anyway. If machinery imported under such schemes is 'additional' to normal imports, it is clear that there would be no balance-of-payments gain, although such imports of machinery are likely to add to the total investment in the country.

Policies to attract more remittances from abroad naturally have to impinge on factors that inhibit their flow or which divert them to unofficial channels. Although it is not possible to identify all such factors, the following would seem to be some of the important ones. Firstly, it is likely that the exchange rate of rupee that an NRI can get for his dollar or sterling through authorized dealers is not as attractive as what he or she can get in the unofficial market or through transfer of commodities. Further, since the usual expectations with regard to the future value of the rupee are adverse, there is an inherent tendency in NRIs to hoard foreign currencies rather than rupees, except for essential current expenditure.

It has to be recognized that in most developing countries, with demand for foreign exchange exceeding its supply, it is not possible to eliminate the unofficial market or the procedure for imported commodities. This is because as long as there is unofficial demand for wasteful and inessential foreign exchange expenditure, there would always be a market for unofficial transfer of foreign exchange. In other words, whatever the exchange rate, a more favourable one is likely to be available in the unofficial market. This fact limits the possibility of entirely eliminating the unofficial market in respect of exchange rate through management of foreign exchange markets by monetary authorities.

REMITTANCES

In addition to normal remittances for expenditure in India, NRIs are also allowed to invest in companies in India. According to RBI data, remittances received from Indians abroad amounted to ₹9.6 crore in 1969–70, ₹7.9 crore in 1970–1 and ₹10.4 crore in 1971–2. (These figures include estimated amounts of remittances appearing under 'unclassified private transfers'.) Investments by NRIs in Indian companies were relatively small, and amounted to less than ₹1 crore on an average during 1970-2.

In view of the low level of remittances to India in the 1970s, the necessity of steps to make the exchange rates for remittance more attractive was considered. From an economic point of view, in several developing countries the most convenient way of providing a better exchange rate for remittances was considered to be the system of dual exchange rate, whereby certain items of transactions were subject to a higher exchange rate on both the receipt and the payment side. An alternative way of achieving the same objective was to include remittance in the existing system of cash subsidies for merchandise exports. While these measures certainly provided a financial incentive, it was felt that the balance of advantage was against adopting such policies. A major problem in adopting a dual exchange rate system was that it was difficult to differentiate between the different purposes for which foreign exchange was purchased or sold. At the minimum, a dual exchange rate system would have also applied to all items of invisible transactions. Similarly, it was likely that a dual exchange rate system would have led to a rise in expectation regarding the ultimate unification of the exchange rate, that is, the expectation that the lower rate would ultimately catch up with the higher exchange rate. Finally, there was the possibility that a higher exchange rate being available without risk, in respect of unofficial transactions, would have provided further incentives for leakage and under-invoicing of exports.

In view of these limitations, the benefits of such a system in India were likely to be relatively small. Given the powerful factors that inhibit the flow of remittances, it was unrealistic to expect transfer of substantial amount of remittances to India even if a dual exchange rate system was adopted. As such, it was considered that it would not be appropriate to experiment with a system of offering a higher exchange rate for remittances.

SAVINGS DEPOSITS

In the 1970s, NRIs were allowed to operate two types of bank accounts in the country, namely, ordinary non-resident accounts and non-resident (external) accounts. Under the ordinary account, balances up to ₹50,000 were free from all control for local disbursement. However, there was no right of repatriation of capital and profits outside India without permission from the RBI. Under the non-resident (external) account, on the other hand, withdrawals could be made not only for local disbursement but also for transfer, in foreign exchange, to the account holder's country of residence or third parties in the same currency area. Deposits were entitled to normal interest payable on different types of deposits, and were exempt from income tax. The total number of non-resident (external) accounts as on 31 March 1973 were 9,718, and total balances were ₹14 crore, of which only a little over ₹2 crore was held by NRIs in the UK, the US and Canada. The rest of the balance was held mainly by NRIs residing in other developing countries of Africa and the Middle East.

So far as non-resident (external) accounts were concerned, these were freely transferable to the country of origin without any further administrative formalities. From a depositor's point of view, deposits in Indian banks were an alternative to deposits in foreign banks abroad. Therefore, in order to attract deposits, Indian banks had to offer the same facilities and convenience of transaction as foreign banks. The rate of interest on these deposits also had to be competitive. As mentioned earlier, deposits were analogous to foreign borrowings, but to the extent that a part of these deposits remained in the country, there was a net gain.

During the period of exchange rate instability, the possibility of providing an exchange guarantee on deposits placed with banks was also considered. The RBI, however, felt that such an exchange guarantee scheme was likely to lead to several administrative complications and possibility of misuse. It was also likely to have a budgetary impact, as the government would have to bear the exchange risk. It was also felt that the inflow of savings as a result of this scheme was unlikely to be commensurate with the costs involved. This suggestion, therefore, was not pursued.

INVESTMENT

Of the different forms in which transfer of savings could take place, investment in Indian industries provided the most promising avenue for attracting non-resident savings. In the 1970s, persons of Indian origin returning from abroad were, on application, allowed to import machinery with a cost, insurance and freight (CIF) value of up to ₹5 lakh provided that these were purchased with the applicant's foreign exchange earnings abroad and the buyer furnished a proper account of his/her holdings to the RBI. Raw materials and components for meeting one or two years' operational requirements, subject to a maximum of ₹1 lakh, were also allowed to be imported if purchased with the applicant's foreign exchange earnings abroad. The scheme was subject to a number of further conditions, such as the amount of shareholding of the applicant and limitation on repatriation of profits. By April 1974, 195 licences for import of machinery worth ₹6.31 crore were issued under the scheme. During 1973–4, the limit for import of machinery was raised to ₹25 lakh, as the existing limit of ₹5 lakh was considered insufficient. In raising the limit it was, however, specified that this concession would not apply to such manufacturing operations as specified by the government from time to time.

It is not clear whether a limit of ₹25 lakh for import of machinery in 1973–4 was necessary. If the permissible industries, in which such investment was allowed, were also socially desirable, and would have been established in any case, then import of machinery by NRIs for investment in such areas should have been allowed without any value limit. The corresponding limit on raw materials and components was also raised to ₹5 lakh.

In order to attract investment in certain critical areas, NRIs were also allowed to invest freely out of their own foreign exchange earnings in priority sectors such as cement, paper and fertilizers. Industrial licences for this purpose were freely given without delay and time-consuming procedures. Non-residents were also allowed to import machinery out of their own foreign exchange earnings under the scheme sanctioned mentioned earlier. Liberal licencing was available for joint ventures with residents in India where total investment in the cost of the project by the NRI partners exceeded 50 per cent.

Investment by NRIs in free trade zones also provided an important means of attracting non-resident savings. In the 1970s, export processing zones (EPZs) were also set up in Kandla, Gujarat and Santa Cruz, Maharashtra. The latter was only for the electronics industry. For various reasons, Kandla did not meet expectations while Santa Cruz performed satisfactorily. All powers were vested in the Board set up for consideration of applications and granting clearance. Such delegation of powers to the Board helped in expeditious clearances, which would not otherwise have been possible.

Significantly, in the Santa Cruz zone, there were a number of foreign equity cases and in three of them, NRIs' participation was envisaged. Each of them had a technical background, and played a role in conceiving the project and bringing together Indian entrepreneurs and foreign collaborators. In new and non-traditional export-oriented industries, identification of exportable products, arrangements for technical know-how, procurement of raw materials and overseas sales played an important role. Investments and involvement by NRIs were also initiated in free trade zones because of expeditious clearance and other facilities allowed.

To sum up, the main conclusions based on the flow of non-resident savings in India in the 1970s, which are also of some contemporary interest, are:

(i) It is not desirable to experiment with cash subsidies to increase remittances from abroad. The benefits of such schemes are unlikely to be commensurate with costs involved.

(ii) The scheme for import of machinery by non-residents should be further liberalized to allow such imports without subjecting them to high taxes. Imports of raw materials and components by non-residents purchased out of their own foreign exchange earnings, for the purpose of setting up industries or meeting operational requirements, should be freely granted.

(iii) Non-residents should also be allowed to invest freely in priority industries such as cement, fertilizer and paper. For this purpose, import licences should be given without delay and time-consuming procedures. The facility of liberal licencing should also be available

for joint ventures with resident Indian partners.
(iv) Investment by non-residents in free trade zones provides a means of attracting savings. Such savings should be further increased.

5

MARCHING TOWARDS A NEW INDUSTRIAL POLICY

An industrial policy is a means to achieve certain objectives in the industrial field. Therefore, any discussion of old or new industrial policies must begin with the country's industrial objectives. Further, India did not start with a 'clean slate' and so it was necessary to analyse its experience with industrial development before working out the ingredients of a new policy.

OBJECTIVES

In a labour-surplus economy like India, there is no doubt that employment needs to be a specific objective of the industrial policy. However, it would be wrong to assume that it should be the sole objective, or that any industrial activity that employs people must be encouraged and vice versa. Apart from leading to production of goods to satisfy consumption requirements, employment must also result in the generation of additional income for the society. Labour, capital and raw materials used in the process of production must result in an output whose value is at least higher than the cost of using the materials and services. Similarly, apart from the generation of income, another objective of industrial policy is to use India's renewable and non-renewable resources in an efficient manner. To illustrate, if the output of cotton and sugarcane, which are required in the production of essential consumer goods, is short, it is clear that any strategy for employment of people that does not take this factor into account is likely to be questionable. Further, another objective of industrial policy may be to generate savings and investible resources for further investment.

There may be other objectives, such as national security, self-reliance, and so on. It is possible that in certain specific situations, the employment objective would conflict with some of the other objectives. In these situations, a balance has to be struck by explicitly assigning politically determined 'social weights' to these conflicting objectives. Neglect of cost-benefit analysis may, in the long run, do considerable harm to the potential development of the economy.

HISTORICAL EXPERIENCE (1960-75)

There is a widespread impression that industry, particularly heavy industry, was emphasized excessively during the early years of industrialization. India's industrial experience between 1965 and 1975, however, does not corroborate this impression. As the then Finance Minister pointed out in his Budget Speech for 1974-5, 'judging by the fact that industrial growth rates since 1965 has averaged only 4 per cent as compared with the average annual growth rate of 8 per cent from 1956 to 1964, the decade since 1965 can hardly be described as a decade of progress in industrialization'. As regards the heavy industry, the growth rate of production in the machinery sector during 1966-75 was 3.3 per cent. This rate does not change even if basic metals such as steel are included. During 1960-5, when industrial growth was consistently over 8 per cent, the machinery sector had shown a growth rate of 19 per cent (13 per cent, if basic metals are included). In line with the growth rate in agriculture, the growth rate in agro-based industries (for example, textiles, sugar, tea, etc.) was only around 2-3 per cent during 1960-5 as well as 1966-75.

It is, of course, legitimate to ask whether a high growth rate in industry is at all necessary or even desirable in a developing country like India. An answer to this question can, again, be found by reviewing the major features of India's economic experience during the 1970s as contrasted with 1960-5. During the period of high industrial growth (1960-5), employment in the organized sector increased at a compound rate of 5.5 per cent per annum. In contrast, the growth rate of employment during 1965-75 was 2.7 per cent. The period of 1960-5 was also a period when the rate of saving (as percentage of GDP) was rising, while it was more or less stagnant in the subsequent decade (until 1975/76).

If there is any validity to the view that rising incomes, rising saving rates and rising investment rates are desirable in order to develop an underdeveloped economy, there seems to be little doubt that a high rate of industrial growth is better than a stagnant industrial economy. While evolving an employment-oriented strategy, it would be unfortunate if the problem of generating an adequate growth rate in the industrial sector is ignored. In a poor society, where agriculture can at best show a growth of 3.5-4 per cent per annum, rapid and sustained industrialization is necessary in order to raise labour productivity and incomes. In this connection, it is interesting to note that in comparison with other developing countries, India's performance in the industrial field has been relatively poor. The growth rate in the agricultural sector of most developing countries has varied between 2-4 per cent per annum, which is comparable with India's performance since 1960. In the field of industry, however, the developing countries as a whole (excluding centrally planned economies for which firm data are not available) have shown an average growth rate of 7 per cent per annum (and some registered a growth rate of above 10 per cent in 1965–75). In contrast, India's growth rates have averaged only 4 per cent per annum. Also, international experience shows that countries with a higher growth rate of industry have been more successful in generating industrial employment than those with lower rates.

There is another interesting feature of India's experience during 1960–5, which needs to be mentioned here. According to official data, the extent of poverty during this period (measured by the number of people below the poverty line) may have increased. This is, however, explained by the fact that there was almost no growth in the agricultural sector. This suggests that, in the medium term, high industrial growth alone is not enough for relieving poverty. Since the problem of poverty is essentially a rural phenomenon, the main answer to this problem must be found in increasing labour productivity in the agricultural sector. It is also likely that, apart from institutional reform, measures to improve labour productivity in agriculture would require massive investment in sectors that are linked to industry, such as irrigation, power, roads, fertilizers, and so on.

The conflict in allocation of resources among these and other sectors becomes severe in a stagnant economy because more resources for one sector must mean fewer resources for another. In a dynamic and fast-growing economy, these conflicts largely disappear because different sectors reinforce each other. In any programme and policy for industrial development, the inter-relationships between different sectors must be explicitly recognized. Just as a healthy industrial economy can facilitate the task of agricultural development, a fast-growing agricultural sector strengthens the likelihood of realizing a high growth rate of industry by ensuring adequate demand for industrial products and adequate supply of agricultural inputs.

In a labour-surplus economy like India, it is unquestionable that industrial development needs to be labour-intensive. It is also true that some policies have given the wrong economic signals and have made it much more profitable to invest capital rather than employ labour. In an employment-oriented programme, these policies have to be changed. At the same time, India must ensure that industrial economy is vitalized to generate a sustained growth rate of 7-8 per cent per annum. The content and pattern of industrialization need to be reviewed with this as well as the employment objective in view.

INDUSTRIAL POLICY

A large part of industrial production—roughly 70-5 per cent—takes place in the private sector. While the government determines the environment in which private-sector activity takes places, and while it can influence private decision-making, it must be recognized that government action by itself cannot guarantee a high growth rate or the choice of particular technologies. The instruments available to the government to affect the behaviour of the private sector in the industrial field are: (i) fiscal policies, (ii) expenditure policies, (iii) monetary policies and (iv) licencing policies. A policy to redirect private effort towards the creation of more employment opportunities in the industrial field must, therefore, impinge on all these policies and cannot be confined merely to industrial licencing policy. It is also important to recognize that while these instruments can certainly influence private behaviour, they are not potent enough to determine this behaviour.

While a few suggestions for changes in industrial and other related policies are made here, these are not exhaustive. Moreover, it is also assumed that so far as expenditure policies of the government are concerned, sufficient attention is given to employment creation, inter alia, through the promotion of villages and rural industries and revitalizing government organizations in these fields. It is further assumed that in giving new orientation to industrial policy, the government moves towards a less controlled economy than the other way round.

INCENTIVES FOR LABOUR-INTENSIVE INVESTMENT

It is a justifiable criticism of India's fiscal policies that most of the concessions that are given are related to capital. The question of relating these subsidies to labour has been discussed frequently, but no solution has been found so far.

It is suggested that both the backward area capital subsidy as well as investment allowances should be converted into employment-related subsidies. So far as backward area subsidy is concerned, the government might consider announcing a fixed amount of labour subsidy per person for the first three years. The subsidy may be related only to the number of workers employed below a certain wage rate. The amount of subsidy may be determined by looking at the average subsidy per person in the past two to three years. This would ensure that revenue implications of converting a capital subsidy into a labour subsidy do not become very large. While aggregate disbursements may be the same as now, the distribution of benefits among potential investors would be according to the number of people employed rather than according to capital expenditure.

Although it is not possible to estimate the likely revenue implications, some rough idea may be formed about annual increment in the wage bill in industry. According to the Annual Survey of Industries (ASI) data, total wages paid to workers were ₹1,800 crore in 1974-5 against ₹1,500 crore in 1973-4. Part of this increment is likely to be due to increase in wages of workers who were already employed in the period 1973-4. Assuming, however, that the entire increment in wages during these two years was due to employment of labour on new projects, total subsidy implicit in the system suggested above would have been ₹60 crore in the first year. If the incremental wages remained at the same level, this would have risen to ₹100 crore per annum subsequently. The actual cost is likely to be much lower as the subsidy would be available only for new projects and for employment of labour at wage rates below a certain ceiling. In any case, the higher the subsidy, the greater is the employment created. It may also be mentioned that given the system of Provident Fund contribution by employers, the chances of misuse of the proposed system are likely to be minimal.

IMPORT POLICY

In the early 1970s, some progress with regard to cutting down procedures and red tape as well as in liberalizing imports has been made. Subject only to the condition that no harm should be done to indigenous industry, imports are permitted freely. Apart from marginal changes here and there, the only basic change that can take place in India's import policy would be to relax the condition of 'indigenous clearance', particularly in products where costs of production are substantially higher than international costs (say, by 100 or 200 per cent). The movement in this direction, however, does not seem feasible, as in each specific case, there is likely to be an inevitable small-scale angle, public-sector angle, employment angle or, failing all this, a strategic angle. Given these realities, although the economy still remains a highly protected one, India seems to have reached the limits of import liberalization.

There is, however, one area in the field of import policy that requires some rethinking. This is the policy of canalization of a large number of items through public-sector trading agencies, such as the State Trading Corporation (STC), Metals and Minerals Trading Corporation (MMTC), and so on. Originally, when most imports were taking place through established importers, the idea of canalization was to substitute the private trader with public-sector trading agencies. However, gradually the role of established importers has been reduced and now most imports of industrial raw materials are for use in manufacturing in domestic factories. By and large, India's past experience with canalization does not show that this particular policy has resulted in reducing costs of imports or providing better service to actual users. Given the improved foreign exchange situation, it seems that the time has come to review the policy of canalization and confine it only to those items for which either long-term arrangements for purchase are necessary or it can be demonstrated that there are substantial economies because of bulk purchase. A critical examination of the past record is likely to show that, on these criteria, only a handful of items such as metals would deserve to be canalized. The rest can be allowed to be imported directly by actual users.

In recent years, there has been a trend towards canalizing items through public-sector undertakings, which are themselves producers of those items. The conflict of interest inherent in this situation, particularly if the concerned public-sector undertaking is also a monopoly producer, is obvious. A general policy decision should be taken to either decanalize all such items or to canalize them only through public-sector undertakings where canalization is considered to be in public interest.

FINANCE

Most industrial projects have to go to the financial institutions for equity or loan finance or both. Smaller projects get their finance from State Financial Corporations (SFCs), while the larger ones invariably get some assistance from all-India financial institutions. Some progress has been made in speeding up the process of clearance and disbursements by these institutions in the last one or two years. It is now necessary that at least all institutions in India give greater attention to the employment effects of the projects financed by them. Techniques to specifically take into account the employment effects of projects are available, but seldom applied. Two steps can be taken immediately: (i) institutions may be requested to value labour costs of workers at 50 per cent of the market wage rate for the purposes of project evaluation. This would mean that, other things being equal, a more labour-intensive project will get preference over a less labour-intensive project and (ii) In their technical examination of the project, they must invariably pay attention to the possibility of substitution of labour for capital and machines in at least some of the operations in the proposed project. In proposals put up before their Boards where government directors are present, this aspect must invariably be considered.

A particular form of control which has outlived its utility or relevance is the so-called 'convertibility clause' which the financial institutions are required to insert for all loan assistance above a certain limit (₹50 lakh in 1975). In many cases, financial institutions hold a substantial proportion of shares, which gives them effective control should they wish to exercise it. A great deal of time and effort is currently wasted in negotiating convertibility clauses, which become applicable after five or six years and in the end are found to be unattractive in any case. This is an exercise that can be given up without any injury to public interest or purpose.

Currently, control of capital issues is vested in the Ministry of Finance (MoF). The exact merits and the advantage of this system of control are not known. A better system of achieving the objectives of capital issues control would be to frame guidelines that can be delegated to public financial institutions. Alternatively, an independent Securities and Exchange Commission (SEC) can be established to oversee the functioning of stock exchanges and to ensure that whatever public purpose is expected to be served by the control of capital issues is actually realized.

6

STRATEGIZING DEVELOPMENT, DELIVERING PERFORMANCE

By 1980, India had recognized the limitations of its post-Independence economic strategy and adopted a 'New Economic Policy'.[1] The New Economic Policy consisted of a shift towards a more outward orientation of the economy, a process of gradually easing government controls, industrial deregulation and import liberalization. While many observers and experts welcomed these changes and attributed the apparent faster growth rate of the Indian economy to them, there were also some who believed these could create more problems than they solved and destroy the national consensus that characterized the evolution of the Indian economic policy in the first 30 years after Independence. These fears were due to the Indian economy's growing dependence on imports, greater vulnerability of its balance of payments, greater reliance on debt and the consequent greater susceptibility in the direction of economic policy to outside pressures. The rising consumerism and display of conspicuous wealth by the few further exacerbated these fears.

The debate on the new economic policy was naturally focused on the suitability of the development strategy adopted after Independence and the effect it had on India's economic

---

[1] The New Economic Policy of India was launched in the year 1991 under the leadership of the P.V. Narasimha Rao government.

development. This strategy was greatly influenced by the Soviet Planning Model and gave the central role to the State in the control and direction of economic activity. Following the Soviet experience, it was believed that the savings rate in the economy as well as the growth rate could be increased if India invested heavily in the capital goods and heavy-industry sectors at the expense of the consumer goods sector. Since the investment requirements in these sectors were high, largely beyond the capability of the private sector, and financial profitability was also low, it followed that such investments were to be undertaken by the State itself.

The Second Five-Year Plan (1956–61) document was quite clear in stating that, 'It cannot be emphasized too strongly that unless steps are taken to augment rapidly the output of the means of production and to build up the fuel and energy resources which are so vital to development, the scale and pace of advance in the coming years will be inhibited.' (p. 28). As for policies to achieve these objectives, the Plan went on to say that, 'In some cases fiscal or price incentives may have to be relied on; in others, a licencing system may be essential; in still others, fixation of profit margins, allocations of scarce raw materials or other regulatory devices may be necessary... If the targets of planned investment are to be achieved, means have to be found to secure that the necessary resources do in fact become available and are not devoted to consumption...' (p. 42).

The State emerged as both the mobilizer of savings and an important investor and owner of capital. Since the State was to be the primary agent of economic change, it followed that private-sector activities must be strictly regulated and controlled to conform to the objectives of State policy.

In this scheme, foreign trade had a relatively small role because of the belief that trade was biased against developing countries and primary producers and the intellectual conviction about export prospects being severely limited. India's First Five-Year Plan (1951-6) was practically silent on exports. It only highlighted the limitations to prospects of increasing export earnings since 'the prices obtainable for exports depend on world factors and may, therefore, be subject to large variations.' (p. 29). The Second Five-Year Plan attempted a projection of balance of trade but concluded that no significant increase in export earnings could be expected in the short run.

The primacy accorded to capital accumulation by the State also meant a relative neglect of public investment in agriculture in the early years of planning. The relative neglect of agriculture was supported by the prevailing view that growing labour force in developing countries could only be absorbed in industry, and that in early stages of industrialization, it was necessary for agriculture to contribute to building up of modern industry by providing cheap labour. A faster development of the industrial sector was the central objective of planning.

This is a thumbnail sketch to highlight the main points of criticism of India's earlier development strategy after 1980. These are: the neglect of exports and trade opportunities, excessive protectionism and import substitution, undue reliance on physical controls and the inefficiency of the public sector.

So far as the actual performance in the earlier era is concerned, the main highlights are easy to recapitulate. There is little doubt that the growth rate of the Indian economy in the post-Independence period was substantially higher than that registered by the country in the previous 100 years. It is estimated that the growth rate between 1871 and 1946 was barely sufficient to keep pace with the growth of population. The growth rate during 1951–80 was about 3.8 per cent per annum. This growth rate, however, was lower than that of developing countries as a group (5.2 per cent). It was also substantially lower than that registered by China (5.4 per cent) and several other developing countries such as Korea (7.2 per cent), Taiwan (9.1 per cent), Thailand (6.8 per cent), Indonesia (5.5 per cent) and Malaysia (6 per cent). Per capita income growth in India was about 1.5 per cent per annum during the three and a half decades after Independence. Population grew at 2.15 per cent per annum as compared to 1.21 per cent per annum in the preceding three decades. This largely offset the benefit of higher growth in the post-Independence period.

Despite the central role accorded to industrial development in India's planning, industrial growth was 5.3 per cent per annum from the early 1950s to 1980. The share of the industrial sector in GDP increased from 15 to 23 per cent over the whole period, but its share of the labour force rose only from 12.6 to 13.8 per cent. The deceleration in the growth rate of industry since the mid-1960s was particularly striking. The annual growth rate of GDP in the manufacturing sector declined from 7 per cent before the drought years of the mid-1960s to only 4.5 per cent thereafter. The growth of agricultural output was also slow. The annual growth of income of agriculture between 1950–1 and 1980 was 2.12 per cent per annum, and per capita agricultural income hardly increased. This was comparable to that of China, but much less than that achieved in some other developing countries. The growth rate in agriculture, particularly food output, was barely ahead of population growth. Throughout this period, despite some improvement in yields owing to the Green Revolution and agricultural prosperity in some regions, agriculture remained an important constraint on the growth of the economy.

India's export performance was relatively poor and the country failed to take advantage of the expansion of world trade in the post-War period. In the 1950s, there was virtual stagnation of exports. Exports grew somewhat faster at 3.3 per cent annually in the 1960s and 7.5 per cent per annum in the 1970s. India's exports were 7.8 per cent of GDP in 1979–80, which was virtually the same as in 1950–1. The share of exports in the GDP of developing countries as a group, on the other hand, increased from 15 per cent of their GDP in 1960 to 22 per cent. The fall in India's share of world trade was even more dramatic—it fell from 2.4 per cent at the time of Independence to 0.4 per cent at the beginning of the 1980s.

Except for brief periods, India experienced continuing balance-of-payments problems, which made the task of economic management and planning extremely difficult. Bureaucratic controls proliferated, leading to excessive delays in approval and implementation of projects and increase in the cost of investment. Capital-output ratio increased significantly. The incremental capital-output ratio increased from 3.89 in the 1950s to 5.46 in the 1960s and 6.04 in the 1970s.

The broad facts stated here are true. However, these do not prove much about the superiority or otherwise of the old strategy over an alternative strategy. Both Korea and China did better, but they followed opposite strategies. The initial political and social conditions were also very different than those prevailing in India. The basic constraint on development was an acute deficiency of material capital and the low capacity to save. Agriculture was believed to be subject to secular diminishing returns. Industrialization was, therefore, essential to absorb surplus labour in agriculture. It was also believed that industrialization, under the prevailing world market conditions and domestic structural constraint, was feasible only if the State took the lead in setting up industries requiring large investment. Reliance on market mechanism was likely to result in excessive consumption by upper-income groups and underinvestment.

The above perceptions were widely shared among political leaders and Indian intellectuals of the time, and the choice of strategy responded to these perceptions. The post-Independence period in India was also characterized by several external and domestic shocks, such as wars, droughts, oil shocks and political upheaval. In defence of the Indian strategy, it can be argued that while the growth rate was slower, India was able to maintain a stable and democratic political system with a mixed economy against very difficult odds. This was a unique achievement in the developing world. India was able to achieve self-sufficiency in food in the 1960s. It was also able to develop a modern, sophisticated and diversified industrial structure. It avoided the debt problem, and it raised its savings rate (from 10 per cent of the GDP in 1950-1 to 20 per cent by 1979-80).

In India's case, in view of the political and social history of the country, a strong central direction of the economy and inward orientation were inevitable. The neglect of economic development by the State in the colonial period had its inevitable consequences. A conviction grew that development was not possible without the guiding hand of the State, and that the State must take on the roles of the planner, the saver, the investor and the manager in order to quicken the pace of development. Over the years, some of the early perceptions about opportunities and desirable policies changed both in response to India's own experience as well as the experience of other countries. There was growing awareness of the limitations of State power, and of the administrative limits to the extension of the State in the economic sphere. There was evidence of vast inefficiencies in the public enterprises and their debilitating impact on the fiscal balance. Unlike India, a number of countries used the opportunities in foreign trade effectively to accelerate growth and reduce their dependence on external capital flows. While trading opportunities increased, climate for aid became worse and political factors were much more dominant in determining the direction of aid flows. Fortunately, India learnt by doing, and there was much greater confidence about the country's ability to develop and absorb technology and compete internationally on equal terms.

SECTION II

THE DECADE OF LIBERALIZATION AND GLOBALIZATION

7

THE GRAPH OF INDIA'S ECONOMY

When a new government took over in January 1980, the Indian economy was in a very bad shape. The government's first priority was to redeem the promises made in its election manifesto—to put the economy back on the road to recovery and self-sustained growth. This was no small task because almost all the sectors of the economy were in a state of disarray. National income in 1979-80 had declined by nearly 5 per cent per annum; industrial and agricultural production had gone down by 1.4 per cent and 15.2 per cent respectively and prices had increased by 21.4 per cent. There was a sharp decline in foreign exchange reserves. Revenue-earning traffic on railways also declined in that year. The output of coal was stagnant and plant load factor (PLF) in the power plants touched an all-time low. The government's first priority was to control inflation, increase production and bring the payment situation under control. It was essential that the misery caused to the ordinary citizen because of decline in growth rate in 1979-80 was reversed without delay.

HIGHER INCOME GROWTH

The Sixth Five-Year Plan (1980-5) envisaged a GDP growth target of 5.2 per cent. A massive outlay of ₹97,000 crore was proposed for the public sector. Additional resource mobilization by both the Centre and the states during this period exceeded the Plan target. The result of this investment of resources reflected in the economy's performance. During the first four years of the Plan, the GDP growth rate averaged 5.6 per cent, exceeding the Plan target. This meant that even after allowing for population growth, average income per person increased by nearly 3.5 per cent per year in real terms, that is, after discounting the effects of inflation.

ACCELERATED GROWTH IN AGRICULTURE

The government accorded special priority to agriculture. Special emphasis was given to the expansion of irrigation potential, increasing the use of modern inputs like high-yielding varieties (HYVs) of seeds, plant nutrients and plant production targets backed by provision of farm credit, necessary research and a positive price policy.

As a result, during 1980-5, the production base of agriculture was substantially strengthened. The irrigation potential was increased by nearly 9 million hectares by the end of 1983-4, and was projected to increase by nearly 12 million hectares by the end of 1984-5. The area under HYVs was raised from 38.56 million hectares to nearly 52 million hectares, and fertilizer availability was increased from 6.2 million tonnes to 7.8 million tonnes. As a result of these policies, the economy withstood the effect of the severe drought of 1982-3 remarkably well. While agricultural production declined by over 15 per cent due to drought in 1979-80, the decline in agricultural production in 1982-3 was only 4 per cent.

The prices of important inputs, such as chemical fertilizers, were also reduced to promote the incentives for higher production, particularly for the benefit of small and marginal farmers. Production of foodgrains increased from about 110 million tonnes in 1979–80 to more than 154 million tonnes by the end of 1984–5. This would not have been possible without a positive response from the farmers to the application of modern inputs in the agricultural sector. This was ensured through provision of remunerative prices for their products. To this end, support prices of farm products were suitably raised from time to time by the government, as indicated below (see Table 7.1).

Table 7.1
Procurement/support prices of agricultural commodities

(₹ per quintal)

Commodity	Marketing Year	
	1979–80	**1984–5**
Wheat	115	152
Paddy	85	137
Coarse grains	95	130
Grain	140	240
Groundnut	100	340

This improvement in agricultural production, particularly in cereal production, helped the country in achieving self-sufficiency in the supply of foodgrains. By the end of 1984–5, the country had over 21 million tonnes of foodgrains in stock, which ensured their adequate availability and facilitated the stability of their prices.

GROWTH IN INDUSTRY

During this period, infrastructure was also given high priority, as it was a prerequisite for increased industrial production.

Besides creation of new capacity, emphasis was laid on improving the performance of the key sectors in the short run. The measures introduced by the government in this direction brought about distinct improvements in PLF of thermal plants, increase in loading of coal by the railways and decline in wagon turned around. The production of coal (including lignite) increased from 106.8 million tonnes in 1979–80 to 145 million tonnes by 1983–4 and 160 million tonnes by the end of 1984–5. Electricity generation also increased by nearly 50 per cent over total capacity existing at the end of 1979–80. The revenue earnings on goods traffic on railways, which had shown continuous decline up to 1979–80, increased by an average of 4.5 per cent per year up to 1984–5.

The improvement in infrastructure also had a salutary effect on the performance of industry. The index of industrial production recorded an average increase of 5.5 per cent up to 1983–4, and the rate of increase accelerated further in 1984–5. Up to July 1984, the general index recorded an increase of over 8 per cent. Important industries such as crude petroleum, cement, fertilizers, automobiles, diesel engines and machine tools performed very well.

CONTROL OF INFLATION

As the common man is worst affected by inflation, soon after coming into power, the government adopted a strategy on the supply side to bring prices under reasonable control. The annual rate of inflation was brought down to 16.7 per cent in 1980–1 and 8.4 per cent in 1981–2. Despite one of the worst droughts in 1982–3, inflation was restricted to single digits in 1983–4, and in 1984–5, the inflation rate was 7 per cent. In fact, by mid-September 1984, the prices of food items were lower than in the corresponding period of the previous year.

These included the two most important cereals, namely, rice (-11.4 per cent) and wheat (-2.2 per cent).

In a developing economy like India, shortage of essential commodities makes the task of maintaining low inflation particularly difficult because of hoarders and black marketers. In order to effectively counter such elements, the kingpin of the government's anti-inflation policy was strengthening of the public distribution system (PDS). Towards this end, a network of fair price shops was set up throughout the country, which provided essential commodities to the common man at reasonable prices. In 1984-5, there were more than 8 lakh shops which supplied cereals, edible oils, sugar, kerosene and some other items. Supply of these commodities was ensured through adequate arrangements for domestic procurement and imports, wherever necessary.

ALLEVIATION OF POVERTY

Several programmes were launched for the benefit of the weakest among the weaker sections, such as the Integrated Rural Development Programme (IRDP), national rural employment awareness, drinking water supply to problem villages, and so on. These were given special attention under the revised Twenty Point Programme announced in February 1982.[2] The IRDP aimed at providing assistance to 15 million families during the Plan period, and the actuals exceeded the target. Similar success was achieved under the National Rural Employment Programme (NREP), which aimed at generating employment for 300-400 million persons every year. The Sixth Plan also envisaged provision of drinking water facilities in all the 1.9 lakh problem villages. By the end of 1983-4, over

---

[2]The Twenty Point Programme was launched by the Government of India in 1975.

one lakh villages were covered under the programme. Two new programmes, namely, the rural landless employment guarantee programmes and the scheme for providing self-employment to the unemployed were started after the announcement was made by Prime Minister on 15 August 1983. The employment generated under this programme was 60 million man-days in the first year and 300 million man-days in the subsequent years.

A number of programmes were also implemented under the Plan for the benefit of the weaker sections and for the promotion of social welfare. These included programmes for the development of SCs and STs, a package of services for persons below the poverty line, provision of large-scale scholarships for students belonging to SCs and STs, and so on.

There was major expansion in the provision of rural healthcare through setting up of additional primary health care sub-centres as well as subsidiary health centres and community health centres. Under this massive programme that covered the entire country, over 1,600 additional sub-centres and more than 100 primary health centres, in addition to over 1,100 subsidiary health centres and nearly 200 community health centres were launched in the first three years of the Plan.

Similar progress was achieved in elementary education and more than one crore children were enrolled in primary schools. Considerable attention was also given to provision of adult education.

RELIEF FOR THE COMMON MAN

Relief for the common man from the burden of direct taxation was one of the important elements in the election manifesto. A series of steps was taken to this end. The exemption limit for income tax, which was earlier set at ₹10,000, was raised to ₹15,000, taking a large number of tax payers outside the tax net. Also, for salaried people, the amount of standard deduction was liberalized, which had a similar effect to the raising of the exemption limit. Steps were also taken to protect the interests of pensioners. The objective of providing relief to the common man was systematically pursued through exemption or reduction in excise duty for essential consumer items, such as life-saving drugs.

Relief was provided to low-paid government employees by compensating for the increase in the cost of living index. While the cost of living index as on August 1984 was higher by 58 per cent as compared to that on January 1980, the emoluments of the low-paid employees had gone up by 70 per cent.

PROMOTION OF SCIENCE AND TECHNOLOGY

During this period, concerted efforts were made to develop a sound base in science and technology and its application to problems of national development. In this connection, the technology policy statement of the government aimed at rapid achievement of self-reliance, promoting indigenous science and technology, appropriate adaptation of imported technologies and ensuring transfer of technology for efficient application of results of research. High-level implementation committee and science programme advisory committee were also constituted to advise the Ministry of Information and Broadcasting to guide the production of science programmes and educational materials for public information.

THE BALANCE OF PAYMENTS

A remarkable feature of India's performance during this period was its success in achieving external adjustment without having to sacrifice growth in GDP. Like most developing countries, India was hit hard by the hike in international oil prices in 1979. India's oil import bill increased from about ₹1,700 crore to ₹6,300 crore in 1980–1. In November 1981, India successfully negotiated an Extended Fund Facility for special drawing right (SDR) 5 billion from the IMF for the three-year period. This provided balance-of-payments security as the adjustment effort got underway.

Thus, India was able to adjust to this external shock by implementing a programme of external adjustment which was an integral part of the Sixth Plan. The programme envisaged emphasis on increasing domestic production of crude oil in order to reduce dependence on imported crude oil and petroleum products. The production of crude oil increased from 10.5 million tonnes in 1980–1 to 26 million tonnes in 1983–4 and an estimated 29.6 million tonnes in 1984–5. This increase in domestic production reduced the oil import bill. Similarly, increased domestic production of items such as cement, fertilizers, non-ferrous metals and steel also helped contain the import requirements of these items.

The total effect of these measures was a faster than anticipated improvement in the balance-of-payments position in 1983–4 and a build-up in foreign reserves. In view of the improvement in the overall balance-of-payments position, the government decided to forego the unutilized balance amount and terminated the loan arrangement with the IMF after availing of SDR 3 billion.

India was one of the few countries in the world to complete the adjustment programme and terminate the arrangement with the IMF ahead of schedule. What was even more important was that India, unlike many other developing countries, completed the adjustment programme without sacrificing growth and also without getting into any serious debt problem. India's success in this regard was commended by international experts. The World Bank in its Annual Report favourably commented on India's economic progress during 1980–5. *Euromoney*, the prestigious economic journal published from London, also included India as one of the five countries that deserved to be commended for sound management of its economy and highlighted some important policy initiatives taken by the government during this period:

> In Asia, Ministry of Finance deserves a share of the credit for India's sound economic performance in recent years. The Ministry's realistic policies, such as, minimum foreign borrowings, helped maintain India's respectable credit rating in international markets.
>
> Government also decided not to draw the last SDR 1.1 billion of its share from three-year IMF facility amounting to SDR 6.2 billion. Thanks to government's cautious policy, India's current account was not weighted down by heavy debt-service costs—the debt service ratio was just 14%.
>
> This allowed India to launch its first-ever international bond issue, in June 1985, equivalent to $ 21 million for the Industrial Development Bank of India.
>
> A record grain harvest also helped push growth up to an annual rate of 7%. India's rapidly developing oil industry was making an increasing contribution to output. Only one third of India's oil was imported, compared with two third at the start of the decade.

Thus, during 1980–5, India made significant achievements in the economic field. The process of recovery was completed and the momentum of growth was restored. Nevertheless, the country was likely to face important economic challenges in the future, which would require strong leadership and dedication. As Jawaharlal Nehru said: 'We are used to facing the challenges of the biggest kind and we are used to winning over them.'

The record of India's achievements during 1980–5 amply demonstrated the resilience and innate strength of its people.

8

SCIENTIFIC TEMPER, TECHNOLOGICAL STRIDES

The ultimate purpose of science is social. Its relevance lies in its contribution to the well-being of society. Science performs this role in many ways. In the intellectual sphere, science embodies a way of life—a rational thinking process. But in the material sphere, its societal contribution is primarily transmitted through its application to the production of goods and services. In this process, scientific knowledge is transformed into applied technology. Technology, by changing production techniques, results in improved productivity and it is through this increase in productivity that societies have achieved rapid strides in economic growth.

History has shown that modern economic growth has been inspired by a rapid and persistent upgradation of technology and scientific know-how. It is estimated that one-third to half of the growth experienced by the industrially advanced countries came from technological progress. Thus, technology emerged as the principal driving force for long-term economic growth.

As early as in 1939, nationalist leaders recognized the importance of science and technology in national development and a National Planning Committee was constituted under the chairmanship of Nehru. The Indian Science and Technology Policy was greatly influenced by the vision of Nehru, who from his early days had an abiding interest in the application of science and technology to development. Commenting on his interest in science, Nehru said,

> Though I have long been a slave driven in the chariot of Indian politics, with little leisure for other thoughts, my mind has often wandered to the days when as a student I haunted the laboratories of that home of science, Cambridge. And though circumstances made me part company with science, my thoughts turned to it with longing. In later years, through devious processes, I arrived again at science, when I realised that science was not only a pleasant diversion and abstraction, but was of the very texture of life, without which our modern world would vanish away. Politics led me to economics, and this led me inevitably to science and the scientific approach to all our problems and to life itself.[3]

In 1951, when the Ministry of Natural Resources and Scientific Research was founded in India to organize and direct scientific and technological research for national development, it perhaps became one of the first countries in the world to take such an administrative step. The Scientific Policy Resolution presented in March 1958 stressed the following objectives of the Indian Scientific Policy:

(i) To foster, promote and sustain, by all appropriate means, the cultivation of science and scientific research in all its aspects—pure, applied and educational;

(ii) To ensure an adequate supply, within the country, of research scientists of the highest quality, and to

---

[3]Nehru's address at the Indian Science Congress in Calcutta in January 1938; quoted from Dorothy Norman (ed.), 1965, *Nehru: The First Sixty Years, Vol. 1*, New York: The John Day Company.

recognize their work as an important component of the strength of the nation;
(iii) To encourage and initiate, with all possible speed, programmes for the training of scientific and technical personnel, on a scale adequate to fulfil the country's needs in science and education, agriculture and industry, and defence;
(iv) To ensure that the creative talent of men and women is encouraged and finds full scope in scientific activity;
(v) To encourage individual initiative for the acquisition and dissemination of knowledge, and for the discovery of new knowledge, in an atmosphere of academic freedom and
(vi) In general, to secure for the people of the country all the benefits that can accrue from the acquisition and application of scientific knowledge.

Actively pursuing these policies eventually bore fruits and educational institutions as well as scientific laboratories were established so as to reap the benefits of scientific progress. The next major landmark in the policy domain was the announcement of the technology policy of the Government of India at the Indian Science Congress, Tirupati, held in January 1983. Apart from reinforcing the above objectives, the resolution specifically called for developing internationally competitive technologies with export potential, energy-saving technologies and technologies that could recycle waste material. As far as the priorities of technology policies were concerned, it called for special consideration to be given to aspects such as employment, energy efficiency of activities and the environment. The field of acquisition of technology, though it called for a selective role for import of technology and foreign investment, specifically stressed the need for absorption, adaptation and subsequent development of imported know-how through adequate investment in R&D.

TRENDS IN INDIAN TECHNOLOGICAL CAPABILITIES

Composition of Capital Formation in India

In the post-Independence period, India followed a fairly broad-based technological development trajectory. The sectoral composition of gross fixed capital formation (GFCF) at constant prices illustrates the evolution of the country's technological capabilities. Through the period up to the 1980s, the share of 'machinery and equipment' in GFCF went up substantially, with a reduction in the share of 'construction'. During the First Five-Year Plan period (1951–2 to 1955–6), 'construction' occupied a share of nearly 62 per cent of GFCF as against the share of 38 per cent of 'manufacturing and equipment'. In contrast, in the 1980s, the trend was just the reverse, with a 35 per cent share of 'construction' in GFCF as against the share of 'machinery and equipment' at 65 per cent.

Some Examples of Indian Technological Capability

Some examples of the benefits obtained from 'technological change' from the 1950s to 1980s illustrate the impact of science on growth. The sharp increase in 'agricultural productivity' experienced in these decades can be ascribed mainly to the shift to HYVs. While there is no doubt that agricultural scientists working in laboratories developed these, their successful adoption was supported by simultaneous efforts in infrastructure development. Similarly, the sharp improvement in life expectancy since the 1940s was because of the successful effort at controlling epidemics using modern medicine, thus reflecting improved healthcare services. Many other examples from the areas of transportation and energy are also available.

By the 1980s, India also had a 20–30-year long history of manufacturing capital goods. Both special purpose equipment for the process plants (for chemicals, metals, minerals, consumption goods, electric power, and so on) and the general purpose machines amenable to mass production (machine tools, transport equipment, consumer durables) had been produced in factories. In the process of vertical integration of manufacture—from assembly stage to individual components—a wide production base had been created. However, the capabilities to make design interventions to further improve the products had not been developed for many kinds of capital goods. In case of certain equipment, the domestic market compared well with those of developed countries; for instance, consumer durables (two-wheelers, refrigerators, etc.), tractors, machine tools, power-generation equipment and textile machinery. Such instances were, however, 'firm-specific' and not general across the industry. Due to the lack of design capability, the changing requirements of the customers and industrial users were not met, resulting in the frequent import of product designs. In the case of capital goods used in processing plants, such design know-how was built through the designing of 'processes'. However, in India, the 'process-design capabilities' had not grown. The initial effort in certain areas was promising. In the steel industry, the then Hindustan Steel had in-house engineering and design establishments. As independent companies competed for jobs with international consultancy companies, they were generally unsuccessful. In 1984, the successful design work done on an experimental high-voltage direct current (HVDC) project under Bharat Heavy Electricals Limited (BHEL) and in telecommunications were widely quoted. But in the mid-1980s, these still awaited contracts from the user sectors. The 'process consultants' had generally been foreign firms, and they had sourced their equipment supply frequently from abroad. Technology for capital goods production could, therefore, mature only in exceptional cases. Such instances were found in products and processes where technologies had stabilized, but the product markets lacked dynamism. A successful capital goods manufacturing structure could thrive only on a sturdy base of designing capabilities.

Technology helps to widen the resource base of the production system of the economy. In India, the major areas where this had taken place by the mid-1980s were the energy and agricultural sectors. This occurred also in relation to the provision of certain basic needs such as drinking water. The successful shift in the technology of oil exploration from onshore to offshore opened up vast resources of oil and natural gas for use. The utilization of natural gas for fertilizers and petrochemicals was possible only because of the shift to offshore production. Natural gas supported more than 40 per cent of nitrogenous fertilizer output and about 50 per cent of petrochemicals. The latter, in turn, enabled a shift in the material base in terms of common usage, from timber and metals towards plastic-based materials. The 1980s, when value added in production in agriculture increased at about 3 per cent per annum, was associated with a sharp growth in electricity consumption by agriculture. It was largely through the shift in the water-lifting technology that paddy could now be produced in the north and the north-west. Even the changes in simple techniques of lifting the groundwater helped to solve drinking water problems in villages with water scarcity.

CHALLENGES FOR THE FUTURE AND POSSIBLE POLICY DIRECTIONS

Effective Patent Laws and Intellectual Property Rights

The twentieth-century Austrian economist Joseph Schumpeter made a fundamental distinction between invention, which is the discovery of new techniques, and innovation, which consists of the practical application of an invention in production for the market. Invention is performed by the inventor while innovation is the task of the entrepreneur. The classic example of this is the eighteenth-century Industrial Revolution in Britain. The success of Britain then did not merely lie in the invention of scientific tools, which may be primitive by modern standards, but also in their commercial adoption. It is this commercial adoption that Schumpeter referred to as innovation.[4]

The existence of an effective and speedy patent legal framework goes a long way in solving the incentive problem associated with any innovative venture. Though the Indian Patents Act of 1970 was indeed a necessary break from the earlier, archaic Indian Patent and Designs Act of 1911, there was still much that needed to be done. A slow process of patenting not only hurts the interests of the innovator but also discourages potential new ones. Existence of loose patent

---

[4]Often the entities of innovator and inventor are distinct and, in such situations, the intimate interlink between invention and innovation marks the interrelationship between science and technology. There are, however, times when the same person is an inventor as well as an innovator. For instance, James Watt is not only remembered as the inventor of the steam engine but also as one who put it to commercial use. Many of the inventors of modern software too fall into this combined category of inventor-innovator rolled into one. Bill Gates is often portrayed as not only the pioneer of Windows, but also as one who marketed it successfully.

laws or their violation, as is prevalent in software piracy, makes innovators less inclined to spend time and resources. This may have consequences on the oft-adopted modes of industrial research in India like imitative research or reverse engineering. What India needed was to stress more innovative research and to develop the intermediaries like patent agents and patent attorneys, who would bridge the gap between the market and the scientists.

The Role of the State in Technological Development

What is the role of the government in the advancement of science and technology in a liberalized, market-friendly atmosphere? At this point of time, the issue may apparently seem to be old-fashioned. Often in popular parlance, liberalization is equated to a withdrawal of the state from the economic domain. However, science and technology is a field where such popular notions may turn out to be fallacious. It is widely argued that there are three sources of market failure: indivisibility, uncertainty and externalities. Knowledge-generating activities such as R&D suffer from all three types of market failure. Moreover, when there is a wedge between private and social profitability, like that existing in pure research, private finance may not be forthcoming. Thus, even in a deregulated regime, the state will have three specific and selective roles in fostering science and technology: financing fundamental research, providing infrastructure and regulating property rights.

EPILOGUE

During the first 40 years after Independence, India made long strides in her quest for scientific pursuit, both in the material and the intellectual spheres. The winds of change blowing in

India, especially in the 1980s, changed the scenario a great deal. It posed new challenges and provided newer opportunities. While there was still much to be done in the policy and legal spheres, the directional indications were right. What was needed was that in the liberal environment, ideas of science and technology were encouraged and those were translated successfully into innovative ventures by entrepreneurs. India had—and still has—the talent, the skills and the resources to be in the forefront of the technological revolution taking place in the new sectors of growth in the global economy. The future was expected to be truly exciting and the scientific, industrial and financial communities needed to make it possible for India to take maximum advantage of the opportunities that lay ahead.

9

OF QUICK ECONOMIC TURNAROUNDS

Except for the balance-of-payments problem, the Indian economy, in 1988, performed better than in any year during the previous decade. Agricultural production exceeded the target, and national income achieved a record growth rate of close to 9 per cent. Industrial production also did well and infrastructure performance continued to be generally satisfactory. The inflation rate was below 5 per cent.

There were a number of policy issues under consideration by the government. Here, a few of the important issues that were expected to be of relevance in the future are discussed.

FOOD POLICY

India was able to cope remarkably well with drought in 1987 because of the government's decision to release substantial quantities of additional foodgrains. This contrasted with the experience of earlier years, when despite large stocks the government was very cautious in releasing foodgrains.

In 1987, while the procurement price of foodgrains was about ₹180 per quintal, the economic cost of wheat was estimated to be around ₹280 per quintal. The government continued to provide complete assurance to farmers that it would lift all the grain that was offered at the procurement price. The aim of the policy was to ensure that farmers were able to sell directly to the roller flour mills (RFMs), and that purchase from the Food Corporation of India (FCI) was undertaken by RFMs only as a last resort. This objective was fulfilled by taking the following measures:

(i) The issue price of wheat charged by the FCI to RFMs was raised to slightly below the economic cost of ₹280 per quintal. This meant that RFMs could buy wheat directly from the farmers and less could be offered to the FCI at the procurement price.

(ii) The FCI thus had the primary responsibility of catering to PDS. In addition, it undertook open-market operations in wheat to keep the market prices of wheat in check.

It may be mentioned that the above policy did not lead to an increase in the prices of wheat products. The crucial thing was to ensure that the FCI operated in the market and kept market prices of wheat in different parts of the country at a reasonable level. Thus, RFMs were actually able to buy wheat at prices that were close to or lower than what the FCI could offer (at existing levels of subsidy).

For the proper management of the food economy, it was also important to have some flexibility in regard to export/import of foodgrains in different years. There was a large speculative element in the behaviour of food prices. By judicious management of export/import and market operations, India was able to counter speculative pressures arising from uncertainty about the crop situations.

A policy decision was taken to provide the concerned department the flexibility to undertake export/import of up to 2 per cent of the average production in the preceding three years. Up to this level, decisions were made purely on economic considerations, keeping in view stock levels, market prices and the progress of the monsoon.

STEEL POLICY

India's steel policy remained basically the same from 1960 to 1988. The results in terms of expansion in production and domestic prices of steel were, however, not very encouraging. As some measures had already been taken to improve the management of the Steel Authority of India Ltd (SAIL), and international prices of steel had also risen, thereby reducing disparity in domestic and international prices, this was a good time to introduce a new policy for the steel sector. The main elements of the new policy were as follows:

(i) SAIL was given substantial freedom in respect of the pricing and distribution of steel. This enabled it to change prices and determine its production pattern according to demand conditions. This policy also encouraged the emergence of black market premium and mismatch between production and demand. The performance of SAIL was assessed by the government periodically in terms of its success in ensuring adequate availability of steel and preventing the emergence of a black market.

(ii) Imports were also regulated through increase in tariffs rather than quantitative ceilings and increase in excise duties on import-intensive sectors. There was pressure to reduce duties on steel items. However, this was resisted in view of the foreign exchange constraints.

FERTILIZER SUBSIDY

After new fertilizer plants came into operation, the volume of fertilizer subsidy nearly doubled. A similar order of increase was effected in 1981. In regard to the prices of food distributed through PDS, the policy of adjusting them in line with changes in procurement prices was continued in the 1980s. This adjustment was necessary to maintain the relative price of food, but an increase in these prices by a much higher amount in order to reduce food subsidy was not necessary.

EXPORT POLICY

It was an established fact that for several decades, until the 1980s, the system of incentives in India was 'biased' against exports. The large and widening trade deficit in the 1980s was a testimony to this fact. It was also striking that the so-called liberalization of the economy was largely based on import-based domestic production for the domestic market. In the mid-1980s, a number of measures were taken that resulted in increasing exports, particularly of labour-intensive products in which India had a competitive advantage. While it was not feasible to change the entire policy orientation (and perhaps not even desirable because of dislocation costs involved), it was considered necessary to devise a framework that could provide greater incentives for exports at the margin.

First, it was recognized that a large part of export production was also industrial production and contributed to industrial growth. This may sound obvious, but the fact was that whenever any proposal for diversion of domestic production to the export market was mooted, it was believed that domestic industry would die and industrial growth would suffer. It was clear that if exports were to increase in the short run, domestic absorption of goods had to somewhat decrease. It had also to be recognized that those who produced for the domestic market were prepared to pay a higher cost in a situation of balance-of-payments imbalance.

Second, there was a need to increase the profitability of

industrial exports (in relation to sales in the domestic market). Since the Budget could not cope with the additional burden of subsidy, it had to be borne by importers who sold in the domestic market.

Third, India needed a drastic simplification of duty drawback procedures. This was crucial because of high import duties. The best way to do this was to have generous 'industry' rates (with as much product differentiation as feasible), and publish those rates. Brand rates needed to be phased out. It was recognized that if, say, ₹15,000 crore was collected from import duties, it would be feasible only if exports were to increase, to pay for imports. There was also a case for introducing some system of drawback on duties on capital goods for companies that exported more than 25 per cent of their output.

Fourth, in setting up new projects, it was essential to look at the foreign exchange balance sheet of the project. As a rule, this balance sheet was in the form of total import and total direct exports. The imputed foreign exchange benefit from potential import substitution was not necessary, as production in some sense could be assumed to be a substitute for imports.

Fifth, exporters were provided preferential access to institutional and bank credits as well as industrial licences.

IMPORT POLICY

During a balance-of-payments crisis, there was no option but to take measures to reduce imports, however painful that was. In the 1980s, India had an import policy structure that imposed quantitative restrictions (QRs) as well as high tariffs on imports that competed with domestic production. On the other hand, the policy was generally liberal and rates of duty were low in respect of non-competing imports.

A further tightening of policy in respect of competing imports was likely to increase domestic prices and profits of domestic producers without necessarily saving foreign exchange. All that happened was delay in getting licences, inflated demand estimates and a large inventory of imported materials.

Therefore, the policy to reduce imports largely concentrated on non-competing and low-duty imports. In respect of this category of imports, action was taken to raise tariffs combined with the tightening of the Actual User Policy. In non-priority areas that were import-intensive and where imports needed to be cut, excise duties were increased, which restrained the growth of demand for those products. There was no point in encouraging the growth of demand by imposing low excise and then attempting to control imports of raw materials and components through QRs.

It is interesting that some of the activities undertaken in the name of import substitution saved very little foreign exchange. To illustrate, it was calculated that domestic production of tinplates, based on imported inputs, saved foreign exchange by only $120 per tonne. Since the raw material was imported at a heavily reduced rate of duty, the revenue sacrificed per dollar saved was ₹40. In other words, the government was providing a direct revenue subsidy of ₹40 per dollar of foreign exchange to the domestic producers. The same situation—though in lesser degree—prevailed in the manufacture of consumer goods and some other items. Domestic production activity in such cases really amounted to a transfer of government revenue to the company without any benefit to the consumer or the balance of payments.

An import tariff structure in which duty rates varied from zero to 300 per cent or more was highly inefficient as it led to substantial dis-economics. As a matter of policy, it was necessary to narrow the dispersal of rates. As a rule, the minimum import duty was 35 per cent. This rate was also used sparingly and only in respect of export or strategic sectors. (A lower duty than this was an open invitation for over-invoicing of imports, as an importer could do so and sell the additional foreign exchange in the hawala market at a profit.)

The main items of import where restrictions were necessary through administrative allocations were bulk items, particularly edible oil, defence and petroleum. The issues involved were difficult, but there was no option of restraining the growth rate of imports in these areas. Necessary measures were introduced in advance rather than waiting for a crisis to happen.

COMMERCIAL BORROWINGS

Even without taking into account defence debt, India's debt service ratio was about 30 per cent of receipts from exports and services. Debt service payments were growing at the annual rate of nearly 30 per cent per year in the early 1980s. This sharp increase vis-à-vis the relatively moderate increase in exports and GDP was the root cause of frequent balance-of-payments problems. While substantial commercial borrowings were necessary to provide liquidity, there was very little scope for financing further investments through commercial loans in the future. Until the balance-of-payments problem was brought under control, it was essential not to approve any projects based on commercial borrowings, unless the entire foreign exchange cost, including debt service, was also covered by direct exports.

The primary reason why commercial borrowings for financing large investment projects were not viable in India was the long gestation period and the relatively low foreign exchange return on such projects. This simple fact could not be wished away.

An important point in India's favour that strengthened its credit worthiness was the relatively low proportion of short-term debt. If much greater recourse had been made to such debt, apart from the inherent risk of such debt not being granted or renewed, the access to other funds would also have been affected. (Incidentally, credit appraisals by banks gave a lot of attention to export growth.) High export growth also gave better access to other foreign exchange funds.

EQUITY INVESTMENT

Foreign equity investment in India was very low, and measures were taken to increase these substantially without upsetting any of the other policy objectives. In view of the overall environment in the 1980s, private investment was unlikely to exceed ₹300–400 crore annually. This was an insignificant proportion of total investment in respect of India's foreign exchange requirements. It was, therefore, decided to introduce a mechanism whereby unrealistic bureaucratic procedures were minimized and approval for foreign investment proposals were given within three to four weeks.

However, it was also important to ensure that equity investment for the domestic market behind high tariff walls did not lead to worsening of the foreign exchange situation. Equity investments by capital-surplus countries were often used as a mechanism for what was technically described as 'tariff jumping'. In highly protected markets like India in the 1980s, it was not possible for foreigners to export built-up cars or other similar products because of high tariffs and QRs. For the foreign manufacturer, it was an attractive proposition to enter into a joint venture with a local entrepreneur to produce these items based on imported components at relatively low rates of duty. Profits derived by investors were largely from the sale of components and not necessarily from investment.

CORPORATE TAXATION

Between 1982 and 1985, the rate of corporate tax was substantially liberalized. Depreciation provisions introduced a deposit scheme that effectively reduced the tax rate by 10 percentage points, reintroduced investment allowances and fully exempted export profits and tourism profits (in addition to all other existing concessions for backward areas). Out of the 83 profit-making companies with assets worth more than ₹50 crore, 35 paid zero tax and declared dividends of ₹86 crore. With the reintroduction of investment allowance 'as an option', the effective rate of corporate tax was reduced to 25 per cent or less.

DIVIDEND TAX

The proposal to abolish dividend tax was also pursued by interested parties after the reintroduction of investment allowance. Apart from technical arguments, the simple fact that had to be borne in mind was that India could not run a system where wages and salaries of industrial workers were taxed, but dividend incomes of top industrialists were tax free. In any case, the effective rate of corporate tax was only 25 per cent at that time and many companies were paying zero tax. Even if the double taxation argument was to be accepted at its face value, the element of such taxation in dividends for high-income groups was no more than 15–20 per cent—and for many, it was close to zero.

EXCISE DUTIES

In the past, India faced demands for excise duty reductions as well. When considering the justification for such reduction, it was important to bear in mind that whether excise duties were passed on or not depended entirely on the market structure and the demand situation prevailing in an industry, and not on government order. In cases where the demand was strong and there were only a few large producers, companies were likely to gain more by way of profits by retaining the benefit rather than passing it on. This was because retention of excise duty concessions gave higher profits on the entire production, and passing them on gave further benefit only through additional production. In the case of man-made fibres, for example, there was no impact on the prices of textiles. When judging proposals for such reduction, it was necessary to ensure that the following conditions were met:

(i) Capacity utilization was poor and majority of units were making cash losses;
(ii) The market structure was reasonably competitive and
(iii) The import policy and import duty were such that consumers had some retaliatory power in the event of producers not reducing prices.

PRICING OF SHARES

Traditionally, in the 1980s, there was a tendency in stock exchanges to undervalue shares. This was not desirable and it was necessary to move to a system of pricing that reflected the true market value of such shares. If underpricing was to be permitted, there should be no preferential allocation of shares in favour of some groups or persons. This also applied to the valuation of shares held by foreign investors. The undervaluation of shares deprived the government of capital gains tax (CGT) and provided room for 'under-the-table' payments to the foreign shareholders. In cases where shares were undervalued, it was essential to make public offers.

10

STRATEGY POST CRISIS

The seven-year period from 1984–5 to 1990–1 was marked by a high rate of industrial growth. The overall index of industrial production grew by 8.5 per cent per annum and the manufacturing sector grew by 9 per cent per annum during this period. Contrary to popular impression, industrial growth was fairly widespread and not concentrated in certain sectors such as automobiles, electronics and consumer durables. These sectors did register very impressive growth, but their contribution to the overall growth rate of industrial production was relatively modest because they did not have a large weight in the index.

In 1991–2, however, the index of industrial production was practically stationary and there was no growth in the overall industrial production. There was a significant increase in the output of several infrastructure industries, such as electricity and coal, but this was more than offset by a decline in manufacturing production. Production of manufacturing industries fell by about 1.8 per cent in 1991–2. Within the manufacturing sector, the sharpest decline occurred in the production of capital goods. This sector, which had shown high rates of growth in the 1980s, registered a decline of 17 per cent. The other industrial group that showed a similar decline in production was consumer durables, where output declined by about 14 per cent.

The turning point in manufacturing production appears to

have occurred in April 1991. Until then, despite the adverse effects of the Gulf crisis in the second half of 1990-1 and a host of domestic uncertainties, manufacturing production continued to increase. The adverse impact of severe import-compression measures introduced after the Gulf crisis on output appeared to have been deferred somewhat, and the initial adjustment affected inventories more than the output. At that time, the expectation was that the Gulf crisis would not last long and that import-compression measures could be withdrawn quickly. The Gulf crisis did indeed last for only about six months, but in India's case, the adverse effects were compounded because of political uncertainty. In addition to the direct effects of an increase in oil prices on the balance of payments, India also faced a 'liquidity squeeze' because of the withdrawal of deposits by NRIs and cessation of lending by commercial banks. As a result, the import-compression measures became even more severe, which naturally affected the growth of output in 1991-2 as inventory levels were already low.

After April 1991, the effects of the import compression were further accentuated by a number of factors on the demand side. First, the collapse of the rupee trade with the former Union of Soviet Socialist Republics (USSR) and the recession in the Western countries affected the overall demand for exports in traditional markets. Second, fiscal adjustment and slowdown in government expenditure also affected demand for investment goods. Third, the increase in interest rates, which was necessitated by overall monetary considerations, increased the cost of investment and private demand for credit. All these factors, combined with continued import compression, had an adverse effect on output.

Against this background, it is necessary to identify some factors that, if implemented, could facilitate higher investment by industry in new plants and technology. Some of these factors are discussed below.

MACROECONOMIC STABILITY

There is abundant evidence from the past experience of India and other countries that macroeconomic stability is a necessary, though not a sufficient, condition for growth in industrial investment. Long-term confidence in the economy is weakened by instability and investment is discouraged and made more inefficient. The desire to make quick gains from arbitrage and speculative activities overcomes the desire to make long-term investments in commodity producing sectors. Instability can be the result of mistakes in macroeconomic policies for political or other reasons, or it may result from events over which the government has no control. Between 1988 and 1991, both sources of macroeconomic instability were present in India. It witnessed two general elections, three changes of government, several destabilizing domestic developments, the Gulf War (which imposed an extraordinary burden on the economy) and the collapse of the Soviet Union. The resulting macroeconomic instability, apart from causing direct financing and fiscal problems, inevitably affected the environment for long-term investments. The restoration of macroeconomic stability was, therefore, crucial for investment and growth. This was also an important objective of the stabilization programme launched by the government during this period.

THE 'DEMAND' SITUATION

It must also be recognized that there is a conflict between policies for stabilization and those for boosting investment.

Tight monetary and fiscal policies are good for stabilization, but they increase the costs and risks associated with investments. A situation of high profits and strong demand fosters growth, while low profits and weak demand are necessary to keep inflation in check. Even though the growth of money supply in the economy at close to 20 per cent in 1991 was high, a number of industries were facing demand problems. This could be due to a reduction in government expenditure, an important source of demand for many industries. It could also be due to greater flow of funds into financial markets as well as the postponement of discretionary consumer expenditure by fixed-income groups in view of the price rise. The collapse of Soviet trade and obligations imposed on countries that were part of the OECD also affected the demand situation for industries dependent on these markets.

In the 1980s, it was not feasible to make a significant increase in public investment. The best strategy for industrial firms under the circumstances was to concentrate investment in areas that were not closely dependent on the domestic demand situation. One obvious area was exports. In this period, the export profitability picture improved substantially; policy hurdles in production and investment were more or less eliminated and many firms acquired a foothold in foreign markets. Another advantage for India was that wage costs were rising much faster in several East Asian countries, which had shown dramatic export performance in the 1970s and 1980s. India's share in world trade was less than 0.5 per cent, which meant that an expansion in its exports from new investments did not necessarily depend on an expansion of overall demand in the world economy.

Much of the Indian industry suffered from obsolescence. In a more competitive environment, only those firms were likely to survive that were constantly upgrading their technologies and output mix. With the virtual abolition of licencing, new firms were likely to enter all profitable lines of manufacturing. These firms also had the advantage of having access to modern technologies and new products to meet all the demands. At the same time, the existing firms had advantage of location, cheaper real estate, a trained workforce and a marketing network.

Another important area with immense potential for further investment, even under conditions of low final demand, was that of 'energy efficiency'. The Indian industry was, by and large, an inefficient user of energy, as its energy use per unit of output was substantially higher than that in other countries. With changes in energy pricing policy and the exchange rate regime, the cost of energy in India, over a period of time, increased at a rate that was higher than the price of manufactured products. Investment in energy efficiency, even under conditions of tight overall demand, was an important source of higher profitability for industry.

FINANCE

A well-functioning financial system is also essential for the growth of investment. There are two aspects of the financing problem: availability and cost. So far as availability is concerned, more savings for private investment was necessary than in the earlier period. The government was committed to reducing its fiscal deficit, which simply meant that its borrowings from banks and households were going to decline as a percentage of the country's GDP. Thus, domestic savings, which otherwise could have gone into government consumption or public investment, were available for private investment. If the government could borrow less, there would be more money available for investment elsewhere. For this to happen, however, it was necessary to ensure that a reduction in government borrowing did not lead to a fall in incomes and aggregate savings. This further underlined the need to create a favourable environment for investment, as growth and savings in the economy could be maintained only if investments grew.

There was an increase in the cost of capital in the past few years, and the long-term real rates of interest (that is, the nominal rates minus inflation) in the economy were about 6–7 per cent. These rates were higher than those prevailing in industrialized countries as well as in some semi-industrialized ones. From a long-run point of view, there was a case for real interest rates to be lower. However, there were two problems in achieving this objective. First, India continued to have a highly complex structure of interest rates, with highly concessional rates. As a result, normal or non-concessional interest rates tended to be higher than they should have been. Second, the growth of money supply was higher than targeted and interest rate policy, therefore, had to respond to the need for restraining money supply.

FISCAL POLICY

The role of fiscal policy in promoting investments in general, or in special regions has long been debated by fiscal experts. Over time, a number of countries, including India, have experimented with various types of investment allowances or deposit schemes. While no conclusive evidence on the efficacy of these schemes in promoting aggregate investment is available, by and large, the consensus among fiscal experts has been in favour of moderate corporate rates of taxation without special incentives rather than a system of high rates combined with special deductions for investments in new plants or particular regions. The former system is less distortional and avoids the possibility of a wasteful use of resources in low-yielding and inefficient activity merely to take advantage of fiscal privileges.

Another investment-related issue in the area of fiscal policy was the taxation of capital goods imports. There was a conflict here too, as India had a well-established capital goods industry which, because of various factors, needed tariff protection. At the same time, in order to reduce costs and make user industries more competitive, it was also necessary to reduce import duties to more reasonable levels. Some balance had to be struck and the government announced its intention to reduce import duties over a period of time. The phased reduction provided scope for the domestic industry to modernize itself and become more cost-competitive.

IMPORT POLICY AND FOREIGN COLLABORATION

Policies relating to imports, foreign collaborations and foreign investment had also been considerably liberalized and there was an extremely attractive environment for new investments. Problems that persisted were sorted out, as the government's overall approach was very clear: both import policy and foreign investment policy were supportive of domestic investments.

INFRASTRUCTURE

Policies for private investment in the infrastructure and power sectors were also liberalized, which provided incentive for higher aggregate investment. In the changed environment, where the government reduced its role in licencing and controlling economic activities, the most important contribution of state governments was to improve the operational efficiency of infrastructure and power plants under their command.

AN 'EFFICIENT' PUBLIC SECTOR

In the 1980s, as much as 53 per cent of the GDP in mining, manufacturing, construction, power and finance originated in the public sector. In 1960-1, the contribution of the public sector to GDP in these areas was only 11 per cent; and in the 1980s, it was about 40 per cent.

With a contribution of more than half the GDP in manufacturing, mining, construction, power and finance (taken together), it was obvious that the future of the economy would be closely linked to the performance of enterprises in these sectors. It was not a question of profitability alone, but also of their contribution to production and growth of investment in the economy. The government was no longer in a position to subsidize their operational losses or to provide adequate resources for further investment. In this situation, their survival and growth were likely to depend increasingly on their own performance. However, it is important to recognize that what happens to public-sector enterprises cannot be a matter of indifference for the rest of the economy. These enterprises are closely linked to other enterprises and sectors as suppliers as well as buyers of goods and services.

To conclude, in the 1980s, the country's industrial future was strong, and by the early 1990s, India was able to achieve an industrial growth rate of 8-9 per cent per annum. India achieved this order of growth in half of the earlier 40 years, despite various problems and several domestic and external setbacks. The key to higher industrial growth in the 1990s and beyond was efficient investment, and this is where India had to concentrate in the long run.

11

THE SHIFTING PARADIGM OF FINANCE AND DEVELOPMENT

Before 1991, the role of the financial system in India was limited and allocation decisions were made by the central planning authorities and not by the financial markets. To a large extent, the financial system also had a limited role in providing incentives for savings and capital accumulation as interest rates were controlled, and household savings were pre-empted through high levels of statutory reserve and liquidity ratio. New banks and financial institutions were set up and the old ones were taken over, in order to act primarily as deposit-taking agencies and providers of credit and finance for designated and centrally determined purposes.

This development paradigm shifted rather sharply in the 1990s when all the developing countries were moving towards a more market-determined strategy of development. There were several factors that contributed to this change in perception. The first and foremost reason for questioning the earlier strategy was the simple fact that actual results in terms of growth of incomes or industrial development were well below expectations. Despite substantial increase in the domestic savings rates in several countries including India, the growth rate of incomes was relatively low. While saving rates were rising, so were capital-output ratios because of inefficiencies in the allocation and use of resources. The period of relatively low growth also coincided with a period of virtually persistent and recurring balance-of-payments crises. Thus, paradoxically, a strategy that was expected to reduce dependency on foreign aid and foreign trade actually resulted in greater dependence on both.

An equally important factor contributing to the change in perceptions was the astonishing success of Japan and the East Asian countries in accelerating their rates of growth by relying on market-oriented patterns of industrialization (with, of course, varying degrees of 'guidance' by the State). Japan's per capita growth rate of 8 per cent per annum during 1953–73 was unprecedented in the history of economic development. No economy had ever grown that fast before, and Japan emerged from the ruins of war to become the world's second-largest economy. Similar to Japan's rise was the record of industrialization in East Asia, particularly in countries like Hong Kong, Singapore, Taiwan and South Korea. In the 1950s, their per capita income or the degree of industrialization was no different from the rest of Asia. However, within a period of 30 years, they were able to catch up with the industrialized countries of the West. A final and decisive development leading to the demise of the old strategy was the collapse of the Soviet Union and the acceptance of market-led development strategies by all the countries of Eastern Europe.

The change in the development paradigm also led to a change in the perception of the financial system's role in development. The liberalization of product markets also required a well-functioning financial system for mobilization and the allocation of savings. Banks, financial institutions and capital markets were no longer seen as mere conduits for channelling savings in predetermined directions, but were rather treated as important instruments for allocating savings among alternative investment choices according to their relative efficiency.

After the onset of the East Asian crisis in mid-1997, there was a further change in the perception of the role of the financial system in development. Earlier, the real economy was supposed to lead and shape the financial system. A proper development of the financial system was no longer regarded as an 'ancillary' or an adjunct to the development of the real sector, but as a necessary precondition for growth.

After the East Asian crisis, the above developments in the real world were supported by findings in the theoretical literature that demonstrated the critical role of financial system in the growth process. The literature on financial liberalization developed in the 1970s and 1980s stressed the costs of 'financial repression', particularly interest rate and exchange rate controls, which restricted growth of financial intermediation and the real rate of economic growth. These findings were buttressed by the emergence of endogenous growth literature, which emphasized the importance of financial market as a source of innovation and productivity growth. It was demonstrated that an efficient and well-functioning financial system contributed to economic growth by raising the level of savings, investment and productivity of capital.

This change in perception was combined with a fair amount of debate on the nature and characteristics of financial markets as distinguished from products or factor markets. Were financial markets special? Did they require a different set of regulatory and supervisory regimes? In the context of globalization, what were the relative roles of international and domestic institutions as well as supervisory regimes in ensuring the viability and integrity of the financial system in a country?

It was recognized that financial markets indeed had certain special characteristics. The most important of these was the large volume of transactions and the speed with which financial resources could move from one market to another and from one instrument to another. A related characteristic was differences among different markets and different types of instruments. Financial transactions could be highly leveraged and the risk of failure could be transferred by actual decision-makers to innocent bystanders.

Another interesting characteristic of these markets was the role of financial intermediaries. There were segments of financial markets, such as stock markets and bond markets, where savers themselves made the decision about when and where their money could be used. Markets were also dominated by financial intermediaries (such as banks, provident funds, pension funds, mutual funds, and so on), which took investment decisions as well as risks on behalf of their depositors. Yet another important characteristic of financial markets was the so-called 'negative' externalities associated with them. A failure in any one segment of these markets could affect all other segments, including the non-financial markets.

Financial markets were also highly susceptible to 'self-fulfilling' prophecy or expectations. Sometimes 'self-fulfilling' expectations could lead to panic as the behaviour of a limited group of operators was generalized. In view of the externalities, volatility and certain other special characteristics, it was generally agreed that financial markets had to be closely monitored and supervised. In view of the growing integration of worldwide financial markets, failure and vulnerability in the domestic market in a particular country could have international implications. Similarly, problems in the external markets could create serious problems in the smooth functioning of the domestic markets, even if the country concerned was following prudent macroeconomic policies.

This close relationship between the domestic and external markets raised the question of appropriate duties and responsibilities of domestic supervisory authorities and international financial institutions. Most of these issues came to the fore in the context of the East Asian crisis and subsequent developments in certain other countries, such as Russia and Brazil. The lessons emerging from the crisis are discussed below.

LESSONS FROM THE ASIAN CRISIS

With much said and written about the causes of the Asian crisis and its aftermath, in some ways, the available literature on the Asian crisis was as impressive as the earlier literature on the 'Asian Miracle'. While the latter had raised the obvious question of what the developing countries must learn from their successes, here an attempt is made to identify some aspects of the Asian crisis that had the possibility of having a bearing on the relationship between finance and development and the lessons that developing countries needed to keep in view to avoid having to go through similar devastating experiences in the future.

An important point to remember in this connection is that even relatively small mistakes in the conduct of macroeconomic or exchange rate policies can sometimes lead to big crises. The Asian experience was certainly mixed, and the magnitude of macroeconomic and other policy failures in different East Asian countries was not the same. However, in several of them, the degree of deviation from the best practices or prudent policies was relatively small. It was possible that they persisted with the defence of the pegged exchange rates for a week or two longer than was desirable, or that they did not take corrective monetary or fiscal action early enough. However, the devastation and the pain that their economies went through because of these policy mistakes were sizeable and unprecedented. This, incidentally, was also the experience of Mexico and Argentina in early 1995, when a major emerging crisis was brought under a semblance of control by a massive international rescue effort launched by the IMF, the US and the World Bank. In all these cases, the proximate cause was the relatively sudden reversal of capital flows on which these economies had become excessively dependent. It had taken a relatively long time to build a climate of confidence and for capital inflows to rise gradually. However, it took no time for this confidence to dissipate and for foreign capital to disappear. It is also interesting to note that the major reversal was not only on account of foreign lenders or investors, but also on account of resident holders of domestic assets who rushed to encash or convert their holdings into foreign currency.

The point is simply that handling capital flows is not easy. While capital account liberalization and large capital movements have brought considerable growth benefits, they have also brought with them greater potential for volatility in asset prices and financial markets, including forex markets. This can cause unanticipated damage to the real economy during periods of uncertainty about the future economic or political outlook. As mentioned earlier, adverse expectations about a country's future during periods of uncertainty can often become 'self-fulfilling'. The fact that such volatility can be aggravated by a weak financial system leading to severe development problems is also to be borne in mind. It must be emphasized that the lesson from the Mexican or East Asian crisis is not an argument against capital flows or CAC.

It is about careful and judicious handling of such flows and the pace of movement towards capital account liberalization for residents. It is also about building domestic safety nets, for example, by keeping the level of liquid foreign exchange reserves high in relation to short-term external obligations.

It cannot be denied that, despite the earlier spectacular successes, the financial systems of East Asian countries were characterized by several weaknesses. Thus, banks were not subject to effective prudential regulation and supervision. Credit expansion in these countries was large and banks took untenable positions in real estate and other unproductive assets, in the process building up large asset-liability and currency mismatches. Banks had also built up huge off-balance sheet liabilities, which moved on to the balance sheet once there was adversity. Cross-border interbank positions were also large. Non-banking financial companies (NBFCs) contributed to the crisis as these were subject to little or no regulation.

Corporates were also highly leveraged. External debt was available at low interest rates and the fixed exchange rates in these countries offered them a sense of complacency, encouraging them to hold large unhedged positions. External debt was high, short-term, leveraged and concentrated in the private sector. Thus, on the whole, there was an inherent vulnerability in the financial sector, and once expectation turned adverse, this vulnerability easily translated into a panic.

Events in East Asia certainly highlighted the two-way interaction between the financial sector and the development and need of an appropriate policy framework. Improving the financial sector's efficiency through market-based reforms was an important concern of the new development paradigm. However, this had to be accompanied by policies, practices and a certain amount of restraints that strengthened the financial system towards stability, so that growth became sustainable. At the same time, proper emphasis had to be placed on growth policies that did not give rise to problems that engendered systemic instability in the financial sector (e.g., a large fiscal deficit).

A related issue was that of striking an appropriate balance between financial regulation and market freedom. While freedom was essential to foster efficiency, it also raised an equally important question of an appropriate regulatory framework given the wide divergence between private and social interest in ensuring the stability of financial system. Hence, a proper system of regulation relating to prudent risk limits, short-term foreign borrowing and the degree of tolerable maturity mismatches in the banking system assumed critical importance for minimizing risks to the stability of the financial system.

The most important lesson emerging from the Asian crisis was the need to be vigilant about domestic and international developments which may impinge on a country's financial relations with the rest of the world. The process of integration of worldwide financial markets has resulted in product innovation and greater efficiency, but it has also made developing countries subject to greater vulnerability and new risks. Strong fundamentals alone could not provide full immunity from a crisis. There was a need to take preventive early action, to build firewalls and to keep some safety nets handy.

THE INDIAN EXPERIENCE

Against the backdrop of the lessons from the Asian crisis, it became desirable to examine the financial sector reforms in India from the perspective of past experience, the stage of development existing at that point and some issues for the future.

India's development strategy for nearly 40 years or so after Independence had placed emphasis on state-guided development initiatives, with the primary role for mobilization and allocation of savings assigned to the state and its agencies. It was not until the Eighth Plan that the role of the financial sector and financial markets was given an explicit recognition in the development strategy. The emphasis on accelerating investment rate through state intervention in a number of key areas meant channelling credit to certain preferential sectors at subsidized interest rates, exercising public ownership control on banks and restricting their activities through policy prescriptions. Some of the typical features that got built into this system were the directed lending programme with high levels of cash reserve ratio and statutory liquidity ratio, ceiling on deposit and lending rate, lending to priority sectors, branch licencing and detailed regulation of banks' loan and investment portfolios.

As far as external finance was concerned, India relied primarily on bilateral and multilateral official development assistance and did not encourage private external capital inflows as a way to supplement domestic savings. The exchange rate was administered and there was extensive control over all foreign exchange transactions, which were subject to approval on a case-by-case basis. Because of pervasive exchange controls, the Indian financial system had remained largely insulated from international markets. This, however, did not prevent India from suffering regular balance-of-payments crises year after year and becoming dependent on aid flows or credits from the IMF.

The financial system, as a result, faced little or no competition, either domestic or foreign, and costs and efficiency of transactions were not its primary concern. Productivity was generally poor and profitability low. The system was also subject to limited accountability. By the beginning of the 1990s, it was becoming evident that the system could not be sustained without a thorough revamping of its operations.

In the sphere of external financial policy, while the exchange rate continued to be market-determined, over the years, there was a progressive liberalization of foreign direct and portfolio investment, and approval procedures were considerably simplified. As a result, by the mid-1990s, there were minimum restrictions on inflow of capital into the economy or its repatriation and servicing. There was also a significant liberalization of policy regarding industry's access to foreign equity and borrowing through long-term debt instruments. The banking sector was given a greater degree of freedom with regard to raising funds abroad and managing their external liability, subject to prudential guidelines. The end result of all these and other reforms was the growing integration among various segments of financial markets, closer convergence of the Indian financial system with practices prevailing in international financial markets and greater opportunity for investors to access both domestic and international markets. At the same time, care was taken to avoid excessive short-term external liability and asset-liability mismatches.

Competitive conditions in the banking industry were facilitated by relaxing entry and exit norms and permitting the public-sector banks to raise additional capital from the market (up to a certain level). While public-sector banks continued to be predominant, the changing competitive environment in the banking sector made a significant difference to banking practices and disclosure requirements.

Prudential regulation and supervision also formed critical components of the financial sector's reform programme. India adopted international prudential norms and practices with regard to capital adequacy, income recognition, provisioning requirement and supervision. These norms were progressively tightened over the years, particularly against the backdrop of the Asian crisis. In the mid-1990s, the required capital adequacy ratio was increased from 8 per cent to 9 per cent in the banking sector. The mark-to-market practice for valuation of government securities was gradually enhanced from 30 per cent in 1992–3 to 75 per cent in 1996. As a further prudential measure against credit and market risks, risk weights were made applicable to government and other securities to take account of price variations.

In the 1990s, an attempt was made to avoid the problems arising from 'connected lending'. There were regulations that limited the exposure of individual banks and NBFCs to any particular borrower or groups of borrowers. There were restrictions on the banking system's exposure to equity and lending against equity as collateral, and its exposure to real estate was very limited. Prudent limits were placed on the financial system and the corporate sector's external borrowing.

In the area of supervision, a full-fledged institutional mechanism was developed keeping in view the needs of a strong and stable financial system. The system of off-site surveillance was combined with periodical on-site supervision for monitoring the risk profile of banks and their compliance with prudential guidelines. The Basel Core Principles for Effective Banking Supervision was substantially adhered to. The RBI's regulatory and supervisory responsibilities were widened to include financial institutions and NBFCs.

As a result of these and other measures, some progress was noticeable in the performance of the Indian banking system in the 1990s. The trend in erosion of profit and capital base was reversed. The net profits of the public-sector banks, as a percentage of their total assets, averaged 0.4 per cent from 1994–5 to 1997–8, against the loss of about 1 per cent in 1992–3 and 1993–4. The gross non-performing assets (NPAs) of public-sector banks (without allowing for provisions) as per cent of total assets declined from about 12 per cent in 1992–3 to about 7 per cent in 1997–8. The improved performance enabled most of the banks to meet their capital requirement from internal resources and the market without dependence on budgetary support. The consolidation of the financial system in the 1990s led to increased resilience of the Indian economy to external crisis. This was evident from the muted impact of the Asian crisis on the Indian financial markets.

FUTURE AGENDA

Looking ahead, it became imperative to continue with the process of strengthening India's prudential, provisioning and capitalization norms and bring them in line with the best global standards. It was equally important to continue with the efforts to introduce maximum transparency, disclosure and accountability, so that investors and counter parties to financial transactions could take well-informed decisions that were based on their own assessment of the market and other associated risks. Stringent prudential standards were no doubt likely to cause some pain and impose greater responsibility on the banks and other financial institutions. However, given the international focus and externalities and linkages involved, the regulation of the financial sector was no longer a matter of choice or that of domestic concern alone. It was likely that over a period of time, the willingness of the rest of the world to do financial business—either by way of trade credits, direct investments or other types of investments and loans—would depend on their confidence in a country's financial practices. India needed to remain ahead of the curve in its prudential management.

The level of NPAs in the Indian banking system was too high by international standards. Part of the problem in resolving this issue was the carry-over of old NPAs in certain declining sectors of the industry. The problem was further complicated by the fact that there were a few banks that were fundamentally weak and where the potential for return to profitability, without substantial restructuring, was doubtful. Leaving aside the problem of weak banks, the NPA levels were still too high in the profitable banks as well. Vigorous efforts had to be made by these banks to reinforce their internal control and risk-management systems and also to set up early warning signals for timely detection and action. In addition, the resolution of the NPA problem required greater accountability on the part of corporates, greater disclosures in the case of defaults and an efficient credit information system. Action had been initiated in all these areas in the 1990s itself, and the problem of NPAs was expected to be contained effectively in the future with the help of stricter accounting and prudential standards.

In order to allow for growth in their assets in line with real growth in the economy, banks and financial institutions were also required to substantially increase their capitalization over time. In 1990, the RBI's minimum shareholding in the State Bank of India (SBI), prescribed by legislation, was 55 per cent. The minimum percentage of shareholding by the government in public-sector banks was 51 per cent. So far, a number of strong banks were able to access capital markets to meet their capitalization requirements in line with prudential guidelines. In the future, some of these banks, including the SBI, were to have limited scope to raise further capital from the market within the prescribed floor of the RBI and government shareholdings. If the risk-weighted assets of these banks were to grow in line with the economic growth, their additional capital requirements were expected to exceed ₹10,000 crore by the year 2000. As against this requirement, the headroom available for these banks to raise capital from the market in 1997 was less than ₹1,000 crore. After allowing for additional infusion of reserve capital through internal generation and access to subordinated debt, the gap between their additional capital requirement and the leeway available to raise capital from the market in the near future was expected to remain quite sizeable.

In this situation, an issue that needed to be debated and resolved was whether this gap should be filled by contribution from the RBI and the government or whether legislative ceiling for capital to be subscribed by the public should be raised. The provision of additional capital by the RBI was tantamount to additional monetization and its monetary impact was equivalent to that of printing additional currency. Contribution to banks' capital by the government had a similar effect, as it would add to the government's deficit. The government, in any case, would need to provide additional capital to weak banks that were not in a position to raise capital on their own. Did it make economic or fiscal sense to add to this burden further? On balance, there seemed to be a strong case for raising the legislative ceiling for market participation in equity capital of public-sector banks.

At the same time, it had to be recognized that, in view of the need to give adequate attention to agricultural credit and rural banking and also to maintain public confidence in the safety of banks, the public-sector character of these banks could not be given up. Keeping these considerations in view—that is, allowing greater access to markets while at the same time maintaining the public-sector character of banks presently owned by the government—it seemed necessary to prescribe a maximum (at a suitably low level) for shareholding by any single individual or a corporate in public-sector banks. The government also seemed to retain the pre-emptive right to appoint, if it wished, the chief executive and the majority of the Board members in public-sector banks.

With time, the progressive liberalization of financial markets and institutional reforms led to growing interlinkages among the various segments of financial markets. The emergence of different types of financial intermediaries, in addition to banks and financial institutions, was healthy and desirable. A diversified structure contributed to greater stability of the financial system in the event of unforeseen problems. However, while there had been progress in developing various segments of the markets, including money and debt markets, the depth of these markets in the 1990s was low and the volumes as well as the number of participants were not very large. An important priority for the future was to develop the depth and breadth of these markets and to allow multiplicity of intermediation possibilities with different risks and leverage profiles.

India also had to devise measures to make interest rate structure more flexible in order to take account of changes in economic cycles and the inflation outlook. In 1997, there were still several constraints which limited the flexibility of interest rates in the banking sector as well as the rest of the financial sector. Given the fact that some of those constraints were deeply embedded in historical practices, consumer preference and public sector requirements, it was likely that some amount of time would be needed to fully meet this objective. However, the process had to begin as early as feasible, so that in the new millennium, India could become one of the fastest-growing countries, with a stable and strong financial system.

12

MANAGEMENT CHALLENGES IN A GLOBAL WORLD

As is well known, since the beginning of the twenty-first century, the world economy has been more integrated, more competitive and substantially transformed in terms of trade opportunities than was the case earlier. While most of the existing trade barriers among nations are likely to be significantly relaxed during the multilateral regime of free trade, the cross-border restrictions on movement of capital, labour and technology are also likely to diminish over a period of time. What implication does this have for India? This is a central issue that deserves closer examination from business managers as well as policymakers.

MANAGEMENT CHALLENGES: THE CORE ISSUE

It is clear that the expansion of the global market and dismantling of protective barriers for trade and commerce create a major impact in terms of enhancing growth opportunities for the Indian economy. While trade opportunities grow, the protective advantages that a large domestic market offered to Indian industries would decline in importance as a source of growth. India's ability to penetrate both the domestic and the world markets, therefore, depends on its relative competitive strength vis-à-vis other nations.

The source and nature of the competitive strengths of nations in the twenty-first century are also likely to be characteristically different from that of the nineteenth and twentieth centuries. During this period, the world leaders in business mostly derived their competitive strength from breakthroughs in major scientific inventions and their slow dissemination across countries. In the twenty-first century, scientific innovations will neither be based on capital alone nor on the monopolistic position of a few nations. Both capital and technology are fluid. It is the disembodied technology, rather than the hardware that is moving faster across countries in bridging technological gaps. In this century, apart from technological leadership, competitive strength of nations would depend more and more on the strategic behaviour of firms, their adaptability to the changing world environment and how they promote their core competence in several spheres. These challenges are primarily noticed in the management and technology fronts.

For countries that are deficient in investment, improving saving and investment performances poses an important challenge in building national capabilities to face global competition. This is a core issue for India, considering that India's investment needs are high in several sectors. The stress on investment, however, has to be tempered with emphasis on productivity growth for facing competition.

It has been an old dictum in economics that factor accumulation alone cannot sustain the long-term impetus to growth. The steady state growth conditions are not solely influenced by how much capital an economy is able to accumulate. The law of diminishing returns would eventually bring down the rate of return on capital and slow down the growth rate of the economy in the absence of productivity growth. On the contrary, long-run growth depends on how effectively and efficiently the scarce capital and labour are being put to use. Hence, efficiency and competitiveness form vital aspects of the long-run growth process of an economy. Technological progress, innovation and human skill development are some of the dominant forces that sustain long-run growth conditions and international competitiveness of an economy.

While firm-level performance plays a critical role in sustaining growth and competitiveness, its effectiveness depends on the nature of public policy environment under which firms operate and whether macroeconomic conditions allow them to achieve the needed economies of scale and allocative efficiency in production. This is why macroeconomic policies and the nature of governance have received increasing attention in the growth strategies of developing economies. It is not surprising, therefore, that much of the current struggle for survival and progress in the economic field is centred on how to improve the economy's relative competitive strength by adopting efficiency-enhancing policies and instilling confidence among investors. As global markets have been increasingly integrated, the risk from non-performance on the policy front is high compared to a situation of autarky and closed financial system. No country can afford to ignore this fact in a competitive world.

INDIA IN THE MIDST OF CHANGE

Even before a new modern nation state came into existence, India had a remarkable history in maritime trade, or what used to be called 'emporia trade' in the medieval times. India, apart from being exposed to free trade from a very early time, also maintained its competitive position in world trade in several goods. India's competitive strength had remained fairly intact even through the colonial era. It, however, lacked exposure to modern technology and a well-organized market.

India generated a large order of export surplus in the nineteenth and early twentieth centuries—the export surplus in some years was as high as 40 per cent of the export values. This was also a period when a slow process of transformation was taking place in the industrial, educational and administrative infrastructures, which eventually gathered momentum in the post-Independence period. While the lack of technology and infrastructure—except perhaps in the railways—stifled India's industrial strength, the policy regime that the country had to face in the pre-Independence period was not conducive to the healthy growth of a competitive industrial sector. Whatever competitive strength India came to possess was due to access to cheap labour and raw materials. In the post-Independence period, the problem of transforming an agrarian economy to an industrial one, building domestic capability in crucial sectors and addressing the immediate need and aspirations of people weighed heavily as a management challenge to a newly independent nation. The role of the government in economic management, therefore, grew in relative importance. Nevertheless, a strong foothold for the private sector was maintained alongside a dominant public sector.

The management challenges in the 1990s were significantly different in nature than in the early years after Independence. The role of market forces in the economy increased considerably with the dismantling of the industrial licencing and control system, liberalization of foreign investment and technology transfer, gradual deregulation of the financial sector and reduction of domestic protection through lowering of tariffs. The industrial sector was exposed to both internal and external competitions. As a result, a process of restructuring started with respect to the firms' core competence and long-term strength, leveraging position, strategic alliances, marketing strategy and R&D needs. This change in approach was seen in both the private and the public sectors. The industry became more and more conscious of building advantages in technology, technical skill and cost-competitiveness. A perceptible difference was observed in the attitude of entrepreneurs and managers in giving importance to consumer preferences, forward-looking planning and devising unique firm-specific strategies to improve the share in the market.

The growth of a consumer-focused management culture has been at the heart of the modern-day economic liberalism. Its necessity stems from the primacy of 'choice' and 'individual initiative' as the basis for improving efficiency. Hence, the role of government management has accordingly changed to a more complementary position of providing macroeconomic stability, protecting citizens' rights and creating equal opportunities.

India's long history of economic management has led to consolidation of strength in many areas. Among the significant areas of strength are the emergence of a strong and diversified industrial sector, gaining self-sufficiency in food, growth of indigenous technological capability in several core areas and a steady growth of higher education, which has helped create a large pool of technical talent. India has a fairly developed institutional infrastructure in financial, legal and corporate governance, which is essential for the growth of markets. On the productivity front, although long-term trends do not indicate a strong position, in recent years, there has been evidence of some improvement. Some studies have estimated the total factor productivity growth in the Indian economy at 2.3 per cent during the 1980s, surpassing that of many fast-growing economies.

There have also been areas of weakness. These mainly relate to instituting a stable and sustained investment environment, providing for enough physical and social infrastructures, promoting competition and demonstrating the required degree of managerial drive that could let the domestic capabilities translate into international competitive advantages. India's share in world exports remains small. Its competitiveness score, as revealed by the global competitiveness indicators, also remains low. However, according to the *Global Competitiveness Report 1997* published by the World Economic Forum, in terms of subjective assessment of business respondents, India's ranking of competitive strength in the mid-1990s was high. This indicated that investors' perception regarding the growth prospects of the Indian economy remained stronger than what was indicated by the competitiveness index.

In short, the steady progress that has been recorded by the economy in the 1990s shows positive indications of India's rising competitive strength. India is poised to take maximum advantage of the greater cross-border flow of trade, capital and technology created by growing openness of world economy. A growing open economy also exposes firms, investors and the economy to external competition. It poses the challenge of cutting through several rigidities that pose potential risk to the industry and the economy. This is where the management challenges face their toughest test.

MEETING MANAGEMENT CHALLENGES

India's management challenges primarily revolve around improving its firms' international competitiveness through strategic orientation and adoption of policies and practices that improve productivity and efficiency in the economy.

The Indian industry has demonstrated the kind of resilience and strength required to withstand external competition. Industry went through a process of restructuring in the 1990s and the managers responded to growing competition with competence.

The primacy of 'professionalism' and 'organizational effectiveness' as national standards cannot perhaps be overemphasized in the context of meeting global challenges. Competition, by its very nature, distinguishes the weak from the strong. With growing openness of the world economy, this aspect will receive even more significance, since what is strong domestically may not be that strong internationally. It is the professional standard—be it in dealing with customers and client groups or improving quality standards and business effectiveness—that the Western countries derive most of their competitive advantage from. Professionalism is a product of both individualist pursuits, such as respect for values and mutual trust, and the organizational effectiveness of a group or firm that harnesses these individual attributes collectively. Improving professionalism and organizational effectiveness applies to both the private and public sectors and this is where our social values will play an important role in shaping our competitiveness in the future.

Another challenge stems from preparing for greater degree of openness in trade and moving away from a protection syndrome. The successive tariff liberalization attempted since 1991–2 has reduced the degree of domestic protection for industry to a substantial extent. Industry has also responded well to this challenge by readjusting to the competitive environment. With global trade integration and obligations under the World Trade Organization (WTO) agreement, India's tariff rates have been further aligned to international levels.

The most important element of sustaining competitiveness is to build internal strength of a company by imparting a long-term focus to its planning and developing its unique strength in the market. This requires identifying India's core competence and taking measures to enhance this unique strength. Given the long history of India's corporate strength, building core competence on the lines of comparative advantage should not pose an uphill task. The Indian firms already enjoy a pre-eminent position in several products. There are many Indian firms that have excelled in maintaining the quality and cost-competitiveness of these products and managed to sustain a long-term domestic and international clientele. In order to face increased global competition, it is important to concentrate on long-term competitive strength and improve R&D, technological requirement and managerial strength towards that end.

Meeting challenges on the policy front also assumes a great deal of importance in a more open world economy. It needs to be mentioned that a firm-specific strategy, to be successful, requires an enabling policy environment that promotes competitiveness and efficiency. Here, the role of the government comes into focus as a confidence-builder, a catalytic agent and a mediating agent. There are three major areas that assume significance in this context. First, in an interconnected global market, macroeconomic policies need to be geared towards reducing uncertainty and risk to investors and savers. This requires ensuring internal and external stability in the economy by maintaining sustainable policies and putting in place a proper safeguard system for the financial sector against adverse international shocks and limiting exposure to risk. The macroeconomic fundamentals of the Indian economy remain strong, as reflected in a relatively low inflation rate, low current account deficit in balance of payments, fiscal compression and prudential norms in the financial sector limiting exposure to systemic risks. These fundamentals will assume much more significance as the world economy becomes more integrated.

The second important area of policy priority is increasing investment in physical infrastructure. It is difficult to think of gaining long-term competitive strength without substantial improvement in the power, transport and communication sectors. In India, there is a large gap between the demand and supply of infrastructure and, compared to some of the fast-growing developing nations, India's infrastructure deficiency is apparent. For example, according to available statistics, in the 1990s, the electric power generation per 100 persons was 9.2 million kilowatts in India compared to 165.4 million kilowatts in Japan, 154 million kilowatts in Hong Kong, 61.7 million kilowatts in Korea and 22.1 million kilowatts in Thailand.

The infrastructure disparity needs to be addressed through both public and private investment. All over the world, the general trend has been to involve the private sector in infrastructure investment. For example, in some Latin American countries private-sector investment in infrastructure is as much as—or even more than—that of the public sector. Increasing public investment in infrastructure and involving the private sector in infrastructure development is a key task for the future.

A third major area of policy emphasis for meeting challenges in the long term is building social infrastructure. India's ability to face competitive pressures in a globalized world depends on efforts to raise productive efficiency of human capital. Sustainable economic growth is linked to the productive efficiency of the labour force which, in turn, is positively influenced by nutritional adequacy, healthcare, educational attainment, skill-formation and other basic needs of the people. High investment in physical and human capital has been the centrepiece of many success stories of the world. The general quality of life in India has improved substantially during the past several decades of development effort. An important policy priority in the next millennium is to make significant improvement in this regard, if India is to remain globally competitive.

SECTION III

INDIA IN THE TWENTY-FIRST CENTURY

13

THE ECONOMICS OF EXCHANGE RATES[5]

Before the Asian crisis in the late 1990s, the widely accepted theoretical position regarding management of the exchange rate was that a country had the choice of either giving up monetary independence and setting up a Currency Board or giving up the stable currency objective and letting the exchange rate float freely so that monetary policy could then be directed to the objectives of inflation control. There was a shift in this paradigm after the Asian crisis in 2003. The possibility of having a viable fixed rate mechanism was discarded, and the dominant view by 2003 was that for most countries, floating or flexible rates were the only sustainable way of having a less crisis-prone exchange rate regime.

In regard to the desirable degree of flexibility in exchange rates, opinions and practices varied. But a completely 'free' float, without intervention, was clearly out of favour, except perhaps in respect of a few global or reserve currencies. And, even in respect of these currencies (say, euro and dollar), concerns were expressed at the highest levels if the movement was sharp in either direction; a case in example being when the euro was strengthening at a fast pace in 2002. Studies by the IMF and several experts also showed that by far the most common exchange rate regime adopted by countries,

---

[5]This chapter is based on the address, 'Exchange rate management—an emerging consensus?' given at the 14th National Assembly of the Forex Association of India, Mumbai, 14 August 2003.

including industrial countries, was not a free float. Most of the countries had adopted intermediate regimes of various types, such as managed floats with no pre-announced path and independent floats with foreign exchange intervention moderating the rate of change and preventing undue fluctuations. By and large, barring a few, other countries had 'managed' floats and central banks intervened periodically. This has also been true of industrial countries. In the past, the US, the EU and the UK had also intervened at one time or another. Thus, irrespective of the pure theoretical position in favour of a free float, the external value of the currency continued to be a matter of concern for most countries and most central banks.

The reason why intervention by central banks in forex markets had become necessary from time to time was primarily because of two reasons. A fundamental change that had taken place in the early 2000s was the importance of capital flows in determining exchange rate movements as against trade deficits and economic growth, which were important in the earlier days. The latter did matter, but only over a period of time. Capital flows, on the other hand, had become the primary determinants of exchange rate movements on a day-to-day basis. Secondly, unlike trade flows, capital flows in 'gross' terms that affect exchange rate could be several times higher than 'net' flows on any day. These were also much more sensitive than foreign trade or economic growth to what everybody else was saying or doing. Therefore, herding became unavoidable.

A related issue, which is a corollary of the intermediate regimes in respect of exchange rates, concerned the need, if any, for foreign exchange reserves. In a regime of free float, it could be argued that there was really no need for reserves. If the demand for foreign exchange is higher than supply, exchange rates will depreciate over time. If supply exceeds demand, exchange rates will appreciate and sooner or later, the two will equalize at some price. However, in light of volatility induced by capital flows and the self-fulfilling expectations that this could generate, there was a growing consensus that emerging market countries should, as a matter of policy, maintain 'adequate' reserves. How adequacy was to be defined was also becoming clearer. Earlier, the rule used to be defined in terms of the number of months of imports. It was increasingly being felt that reserves should at least be sufficient to cover likely variations in capital flows or the 'liquidity at risk'. (However, there was no consensus on the upper limit for reserves. Even after an 'adequate' level was reached, reserves may have continued to increase if capital inflows were strong and central banks decided to intervene in order to moderate the degree of appreciation.)

To sum up, it seemed that the debate on appropriate policies relating to forex markets had converged around some generally accepted views. Among these were: (i) exchange rates should be flexible and not fixed or pegged; (ii) countries should be able to intervene or manage exchange rates—to at least some degree—if movements are believed to be destabilizing in the short run and (iii) reserves should be sufficient to take care of fluctuations in capital flows and 'liquidity at risk'.

There were still some issues of practical importance in the management of forex markets in India that figured prominently in the media and expert commentary. A frequently discussed question was about CAC, that is, when was India going to move to full CAC? India had liberalized and deregulated a whole host of capital account transactions. It was probably fair to say that most transactions required, for business or personal convenience, the rupee—which, for all practical purposes, was convertible. In cases where specific permission was required for transactions above a high monetary ceiling, this permission was also generally forthcoming. It was also the declared policy of the government and the RBI to continue with this process of liberalization. In this sense, CAC continued to be a desirable objective for all investment- and business-related transactions and India was expected to be able to achieve this objective in not too distant a future.

There were, however, two areas where India needed to be extremely cautious—one was unlimited access to short-term external commercial borrowing to meet working capital and other domestic requirements and the other concerned the question of providing unrestricted freedom to domestic residents to convert their domestic bank deposits and idle assets (such as, real estate) in response to market developments or exchange rate expectations.

In respect of short-term external commercial borrowings, there was already a strong international consensus that emerging markets should keep such borrowings relatively small in relation to their total external debt or reserves. Many of the financial crises in the 1990s occurred because the short-term debt was excessive. When times were good, such debt was easily accessible. The position, however, changed dramatically in times of external pressure. All creditors who could redeem the debt did so within a very short period, causing extreme domestic financial vulnerability. The occurrence of such a possibility had to be avoided and India had followed the policy of keeping access to short-term debt limited at all times—good and bad.

So far as the free convertibility of domestic assets by residents was concerned, the issues were somewhat more fundamental. It had to do with the differential impact of 'stock' and 'flows' in determining external vulnerability. The day-to-day movement in exchange rates was determined by 'flows' of funds, that is, by demand and supply of spot or forward transactions in the market. Now, suppose the exchange rate was depreciating unduly sharply (for whatever reasons) and was expected to continue to do so for the near future. Further, suppose that domestic residents, therefore, decided that they should convert a part or whole of their stock of domestic assets from domestic currency to foreign currency. This was financially desirable, as the domestic value of their converted assets was expected to increase because of anticipated depreciation. And, if a large number of residents decided to do so simultaneously within a short period of time, this expectation would become self-fulfilling. A severe external crisis was then unavoidable.

Consider India's case, for example. Its reserves were high and exchange rate movements were, by and large, orderly. Now, suppose there was an event that created external uncertainty, for example, what actually happened at the time of Kargil, or the imposition of sanctions after Pokhran, or the oil crises earlier. At these times, the multiple of domestic deposits over reserves was several times higher than in a stable situation. One can imagine what would have happened to India's external situation, if within a very short period, domestic residents had decided to rush to their neighbourhood banks and convert a significant part of these deposits into sterling, euro or dollar.

No emerging market exchange rate system can cope with this kind of contingency. This may be unlikely, but it must be factored in while deciding on a long-term policy of free convertibility of 'stock' of domestic assets. Incidentally, this kind of eventuality is less likely to occur in respect of industrial countries with international currencies such as the euro or dollar, which are held by banks, corporates and other entities as part of their long-term global asset portfolio (as distinguished from emerging market currencies in which banks and other intermediaries take a daily long or short position for purposes of currency trade).

In the early 2000s, another issue that figured prominently in the debate was one related to foreign exchange reserves. As was well known, India's foreign exchange reserves had increased substantially in the past few years, and were now one of the largest among developing countries. The fact that most of the constituents of India's balance of payments were showing positive trends was a reflection of the increasing competitiveness of the Indian economy and strong confidence of the international community in its growth potential. For the first time after Independence, the fragility of the balance of payments was no longer a concern of policymakers. This was a highly positive development and regarded as such by people at large.

Nevertheless, expert commentators had expressed two concerns—one was about the 'cost' of additional reserves, and the other was the impact of 'arbitrage' in inducing higher inflows. So far as the cost of additional reserves was concerned, it needed to be borne in mind that the bulk of additions to reserves in the recent period was on account of non-debt creating inflows. India's total external debt, including NRI deposits, had increased relatively slowly as compared with the increase in reserves, particularly in the preceding couple of years. In fact, India pre-paid more than $3 billion of external debt in 2002. It may also be mentioned that rates of interest paid on NRI deposits and multilateral loans in foreign currency were in line with or lower than the prevailing international interest rates.

On NRI rupee deposits, interest rates in the preceding couple of years had been in line with interest rates on deposits by residents and were currently even lower than domestic interest rates. So far as other non-debt creating inflows (that is, FDI, portfolio investment or remittances) were concerned, such inflows were commercial in nature and enjoyed the same returns and risks, including exchange rate risk, as any other form of domestic investment or remittance by residents. The cost to the country of such flows was the same, irrespective of whether they added to reserves or were matched by equivalent foreign currency outflow on account of higher imports or investments abroad by residents. On the whole, it seemed that the 'cost' of additional reserves was really a non-issue from a broader macroeconomic point of view.

The Indian interest rates, over time, have been substantially higher than those prevailing in the US, Europe, the UK or Japan. This provided an 'arbitrage' opportunity to the holder of liquid assets abroad, who may take advantage of higher domestic interest rates in India leading to a possible short-term upsurge in capital flows. However, there were several considerations that indicated that 'arbitrage' per se was unlikely to have been a primary factor in influencing remittances or investment decisions by NRIs or foreign entities in the recent period. Among these were:

(i) The minimum period of deposits by NRIs in Indian rupees in 2003 was one year and the interest rate on such deposits was subject to a ceiling rate of 2.5 per cent over the London Interbank Offered Rate (Libor). This was broadly in line with one-year forward premium on the dollar in the Indian market (interest rates on dollar deposits by NRIs were actually below Libor).

(ii) Outside of NRI deposits, investments by foreign institutional investors (FIIs) in debt funds in 2003, was subject to an overall cap of only $1 billion in the aggregate. In other words, the possibility of arbitrage by FIIs in respect of pure debt funds was limited to this low figure of $1 billion (excluding investments in a mix of equity and debt funds).

(iii) Interest rates and yields on liquid securities were highly variable abroad as well as in India and the differential between the two rates could change very sharply within a short time depending on market expectations. It is interesting to note that the yield on 10-year Treasury bills in the US had risen to about 4.4 per cent as compared with 5.6 per cent on government bonds of similar maturity in India at the end of July 2003. Taking into account the forward premia on dollars and yield fluctuations, except for a brief period, there was likely to be little incentive to send large amounts of capital to India merely to take advantage of the interest rate differential.

On the whole, it seemed that external flows into India had been motivated by factors other than pure arbitrage. Figures on sources of reserve accretion available up to the end of last year (2002–3) confirm this view. It is also pertinent to note that domestic interest rates among industrial countries also varied considerably. For example, in Japan, they were close to zero. In the UK, they were above 4 per cent, and in the US about 1.5 per cent. There was no evidence that capital had been moving out of the US to the UK or Europe merely on account of interest rate differential. Within a certain low range, capital flows were likely to be more influenced by outlook for growth and inflation than pure arbitrage even among industrial countries.

Another point that has been forcefully put forward by several experts in the context of rising reserves is that India should use its reserves to increase investment for further development rather than keeping them as liquid assets. It was argued that it was paradoxical for a developing country to have higher foreign inflows of capital and thereby add to its reserves, rather than use foreign savings to enhance the rate of investment in the economy.

In principle, this point was valid. There was no doubt that in the present situation, maximum support had to be given to increasing the level of investment, particularly in the infrastructure sector. It was for this reason that the RBI in the recent period had been following a soft interest rate policy in an environment of low inflation. However, at the same time, it must be emphasized that there was very little that the RBI (or, for that matter, the government) could directly do to use additional reserves for investment. The equivalent rupee resources had already been released by the RBI to recipients of foreign exchange, and equivalent rupee liquidity had already been created. The decision on whether to invest, consume or deposit these additional rupee resources lay with recipients, and not with the RBI.

One issue that was of considerable interest in India in the context of high and rising reserves, easy liquidity, low interest rates and the weakening dollar was: what should be the correct or right policy stance for the management of exchange rate in India in the present environment? In the RBI's periodic credit policy statements, as well as other public statements, the RBI had highlighted the main pillars of its strategy for the management of the exchange rate. These were: the RBI did not have a fixed 'target' for the exchange rate which it tried to defend or pursue over time; the RBI was prepared to intervene in the market to dampen excessive volatility as and when necessary; the RBI's purchases or sales of foreign currency were undertaken through a number of banks and were generally discrete and smooth; and market operations and exchange rate movement were to be, in principle, transaction-oriented rather than speculative.

It is perhaps fair to say that the actual results of the exchange rate policy followed by the RBI, since the Asian crisis in particular, had been highly positive. In addition to sharp increase in reserves and generally 'orderly' movements in exchange rates with lower volatility, the confidence level of domestic and foreign investors in the Indian external sector policies was strong. India's policies were also described by the IMF as being 'comparable to the global best practices' in a study of 20 select industrial and developing countries in 2002. Interestingly, a leading global news agency, in an international journal, had also described India's currency model as being 'ideal' for Asia. India was one of the very few developing countries that had set up its own clearing house for dollar-rupee transaction with the concurrence of the Federal Reserve System, New York.

In 2003, however, when the dollar was depreciating against major currencies and the rupee was appreciating against the dollar (albeit slowly), a number of suggestions were made by experts and others calling for a shift in the RBI's exchange rate policies. Three alternative approaches were suggested for consideration. These were:

(i) One view advanced by several distinguished economists was that the rupee should be allowed to appreciate freely in line with market trends. According to this view, there was no strong case for the RBI's further intervention, as reserves were already very high. The RBI's purchases created substantial additional domestic liquidity, which could have been destabilizing in the long run. There was also no evidence, in their opinion, that unconstrained appreciation or volatility would affect growth prospects or lead to any other macroeconomic problem.

(ii) An exactly opposite view, which, among others, had been articulated by an important all-India industry association, was that the RBI should intervene more aggressively in the market to further reduce the degree of appreciation. The main argument in favour of this view was that India must maintain its global 'competitiveness', particularly in relation to China.

(iii) A third view was that the RBI should pursue what it had referred to as a policy of 'calculated volatility'. It had been argued that the existing policy of controlled volatility had provided virtually riskless gain to market participants since the rupee has been expected to appreciate substantially and continuously during 2002–3. According to this view, in order to prevent excessive capital inflows during this period, the RBI should allow the exchange rate to 'overshoot' whatever is regarded as the targeted exchange rate by traders in the foreign exchange market. In essence, this proposal was akin to a policy of (announced or unannounced) fixed exchange rate within a wider band.

In theory, each of the above alternative approaches had some merit. However, it was not entirely clear that they could be put into practice without causing substantial instability or uncertainty and possible emergence of macroeconomic problems that were worse than what they were trying to solve. An implicit assumption in two of the above alternatives was that there was a level at which, after initial fast appreciation, the exchange rate would either stabilize or turn around. A further implicit assumption was that the level (whatever it was) was either already known or would become known to the market as it was reached.

The RBI's past experience did not suggest that these assumptions were valid. It would be recalled that there had been periods when rupee exchange rates were relatively more volatile and movements were sharper. However, during periods of sharper appreciation, instead of inflows declining and demand for foreign currency rising, it was noticed that actual market behaviour was the opposite. The opposite was also true during periods of sharp depreciation. Exchange rate expectations had their own momentum and were often self-fulfilling. There must, of course, be a level where these expectations would reverse. However, if that level, because of 'momentum' trading in imperfect and thin markets happened to be significantly out of line with 'fundamentals', considerable instability and substantial overvaluation (or under valuation) may result. Such an outcome was expected to do more harm than good to the confidence in a country's exchange rate system.

The third suggestion to hold the rates at existing levels and to not allow it to appreciate any further, even if inflows were strong, was also likely to be unsustainable over any length of time. It virtually amounts to adopting a 'fixed' or a near-fixed exchange rate system with a floor. Past experience suggested that this system could work well, as it did in East Asia prior to the crisis, when the economy was doing well and inflows were strong, but it came under extreme pressure when there were unfavourable domestic or external developments. Abandonment of a system of 'fixed' exchange rates (or a system with a known floor) then became unavoidable. Such a change, when it occurred under pressure, could result in considerable instability, which was likely to be spread over a fairly long period. At the end of this process, the country then had no option but to revert to a more flexible exchange rate system.

It was by no means a mere coincidence that all countries affected by external crises in the 1990s had a fixed or near-fixed exchange rate system. China was an exception to the rule in view of its persistent trade surpluses over a long period combined with very high levels of FDI. China's special characteristics, however, were difficult to replicate in other emerging markets with lower volume of trade and foreign investment.

The desirability of maintaining the overall competitiveness of an economy could hardly be questioned. However, the long-run competitiveness of an economy needed to be measured in relation to a multiple currency basket as well as to exchange rate movements in major trading partners over a reasonably long period of time. Exchange rate fluctuations among major currencies were now an everyday fact of life, and it was important for all entities with foreign exchange exposures to resort to 'hedging' with appropriate risk management of assets and liabilities.

On balance, the benefits of the suggested alternatives to the present system were not very clear. The existing system was by no means an ideal one. However, like the old cliché about virtues of democracy, it was probably better in the long run than all the available alternatives. In view of the behavioural and market complexities in this area, as well as multiple economic policy objectives, solutions that seem 'ex ante' optimal could turn out to be disastrous 'ex-post' (after the event).

14

IS THE PARLIAMENT BEING SILENCED?

The Parliament of India is truly representative of the vast economic, social, regional and religious diversity of India. All income classes—from the richest industrialist to the poorest farmer—are represented. All castes and all regions find equitable representation depending on their size, population and electoral popularity. Members belong to different religions and can openly and freely espouse their beliefs, irrespective of their numbers. In the midst of this great diversity, there is also unity. Every member has a single vote and an equal right to intervene in the debate independently or on behalf of a party. The time and space allotted to party or non-party members is also equitably distributed depending on their numbers. Ministers speak on behalf of the government, but have no special privileges or ostentatious perquisites or attendants inside the House. Any member is free to interrupt, shout or otherwise disrupt the proceedings of the House, irrespective of seniority, and is subject only to the directions of the Chair inside the House. There is discussion and debate on important matters raised by the members and there may be strong political differences among the parties within and outside the government, but as it happens, most legislative proposals and official resolutions are normally adopted without dissent.

While all this is true, over the years, there has been a subtle change in the role of the Parliament below the surface, which is not evident at first glance. All the citizens who follow the news in the media or who watch parliamentary proceedings are aware of, and perhaps disappointed with, frequent disruptions that now occur in the two Houses. The concern with the functioning of India's Parliament and state legislatures was also voiced by the National Commission to Review the working of the Constitution (2002):

> If there is a sense of unease with the way the Parliament and the State legislatures are functioning, it may be due to a decline in recent years in both the quantity and quality of work done by them. Over the years the number of days on which the houses sit to transact legislative and other business has come down very significantly. Even the relatively fewer days on which the houses meet are often marked by unseemly incidents, including use of force to intimidate opponents, shouting and shutting out of debate and discussion resulting in frequent adjournments. There is increasing concern about the decline of Parliament's falling standards of debate, erosion of the moral authority and prestige of the supreme tribune of the people.

The diminishing role of the Parliament in the conduct of national affairs is actually broader than what has been highlighted by the Commission. In recent years, there is increasing acceptance by political leaders of the frequent violation of democratic norms and conventions in the political decision-making process. As a result, there is a possible threat to the preservation of the cherished goals of 'Unity in Diversity', which was an important gift to the nation from leaders like Mahatma Gandhi and Nehru in the early years of independent India. Some signs of the increasing divide in the national mainstream have been evident. In 2006, as many as 160 districts of India were under the influence of Naxalites and functioned largely outside the control of state governments. As the then prime minister observed during the meeting of chief ministers on Naxalism:

> Naxalism is the single biggest internal security challenge ever faced by our country... ...the movement has gained in strength and now spread to over 160 districts all over the country... ...the extremists are trying to establish 'liberation zones' in core areas where they are dispensing basic state functions of administration, policing and justice.

To what extent the growing power of militant movements reflect the weakness of the State is a moot question. It is a fact that in several states where lawlessness has spread in a large number of districts, administration has been extremely weak. Political leadership has been ineffective and there have been frequent and arbitrary transfers of senior police officers and other district officials. The duality of India is also evident in the increasing income disparities among the people—the vast contrast between India's rising global economic position, as reflected in the large number of Indians in the list of world's billionaires, and the deteriorating conditions in its rural areas, where more than 70 per cent of its citizens live. This divide is also reflected in the divisiveness at the highest levels of government, where ministers and leaders belonging to different parties are inclined to follow their own agenda rather than a collective and shared vision for the nation's future.

In the following sections, some instances are highlighted where the proceedings of the Parliament, including its silences, posed serious challenges to the functioning of India's democracy as a unifying force among people with a diversity of interests, identities and outlooks. Incidentally, what is said below largely reflects the happenings in the Upper House of the Indian Parliament, the Rajya Sabha. It has also lost its separate identity, as what happens in this House largely reflects the positions taken by the different parties in the Lok Sabha, the House of the People. If the Lok Sabha is disrupted, so is the Rajya Sabha, and vice versa. If a bill is passed in the Lok Sabha without discussion because of disruptions or because sufficient time is not available for discussion, the Rajya Sabha is also likely to follow suit.

TAXATION WITHOUT REPRESENTATION

In India's long and distinguished parliamentary history, the events that took place between 18 March and 22 March, during the Budget session of 2006, were perhaps unique. During the course of these five days, a number of unexpected decisions were announced by the government regarding the business agendas of the two Houses, which were passively accepted by both the Houses. These decisions involved a major change in the established procedure for consideration of the Budget, a drastic revision in the business of the two Houses without adequate notice and a sudden adjournment of the Parliament sine die (followed by a reversal of this decision again a few days later). The passive and ready acceptance by the Parliament, the supreme institution of India's democracy, of these decisions that were contrary to well-established parliamentary conventions, had serious implications for the future. Hence, it is worth evaluating the proceedings of these five days in detail here.

As per the usual procedure, the Budget session of the Parliament for 2006 was convened by the President to meet in two parts—from 16 February to 17 March and again from 3 April to 28 April. However, on 7 March 2006, in view of the elections announced by the Election Commission in five states over the months of April and May, it was decided to have a longer interval between the two parts of the Budget session. The dates announced earlier for the two parts of the session were changed, and it was decided to hold the first session from 16 February to 22 March and the second session from 10 May to 23 May.

It will be recalled that, according to Rules 272 and 331G of the Rules of Procedure and Conduct of Business in the Rajya Sabha and the Lok Sabha respectively, it is mandatory for the demands for grants of the ministries and departments of the Government of India to be examined by the concerned standing committees of the Parliament (which were set up in 1993). The standing committees consist of members of both the Houses of the Parliament. The agenda and the meetings of the committees are conducted by a chairperson, who is usually a senior member of one of the Houses. The examination of the Budget grants by these committees allows the members, belonging to both Houses and to different parties, to question the senior representatives of the ministries or departments and also to hear and examine other witnesses, including members of NGOs and experts.

In order to allow the standing committees sufficient time for careful consideration of the Budget demands, it has also been the convention for the Houses of the Parliament to adjourn for about a fortnight between the two parts of the Budget session. In 2006, as it happened, after the changes in the dates of the two parts of the Budget session was announced on 7 March, a controversy arose about the definition of the so-called 'office of profit'. Some members were alleged to have been appointed to such offices by state and Central governments, which is not permissible under the Constitution. One well-known member was also disqualified as a Member of Parliament (MP) on these grounds by the President on the advice of the Election Commission.

On 18 March 2006, all of a sudden the government decided to introduce a motion in the Rajya Sabha for the suspension of Rule 272 (and a similar motion for the suspension of the relevant rule in the Lok Sabha). The motion to suspend consideration of Budget demands by the standing committees was moved and adopted without discussion in the two Houses on the same day. With the suspension of consideration by the standing committees, the ground was cleared for the adoption of the Budget as well as the Finance Bill in the first part of the session itself.

Rule 272 was suspended in the Rajya Sabha on 18 March and Rule 331G was suspended in the Lok Sabha on the previous day. There was no session of Parliament on 19 March, which was a Sunday. On Monday, 20 March, the consideration of the Budget demand for grants (or the appropriation bill) as passed by the Lok Sabha on 18 March, was listed in the revised list of business in the Rajya Sabha. The budget appropriations were considered and approved by the House on the same day.

Developments in the Parliament on Wednesday, 22 March, were, however, even more extraordinary and unexpected—and, in some sense, bizarre. Before the Parliament met in the morning on that day, there was a strong rumour that the ruling coalition was considering exempting certain offices from the purview of the proposed offices of profit legislation by issuing an ordinance after the first part of the Budget session ended in the evening.

As a mark of protest, the opposition parties decided to disrupt the Parliament on 22 March and not allow any listed business to be considered (the Union Budget had already been passed on the previous day). After an obituary reference, which lasted for about four minutes when the House met at

11.00 a.m., in view of the shouting by some of its members, it was decided by the chairman of the Rajya Sabha to adjourn the House for 20 minutes (from 11.10 a.m. to 11.30 a.m.). The House met as scheduled, but was again adjourned after four minutes due to disruption and was asked to meet again at 1.00 p.m. However, during those four minutes, more than a hundred papers, including the annual reports of public-sector organizations, outcome and performance budgets, reports of actions taken and the notifications issued by various departments of the government were laid on the table of the House by a dozen ministers in the midst of pandemonium. After assembling at 1.00 p.m., the House had to be adjourned for the third time without conducting any business. It was asked to reassemble at 2.00 p.m.

The House met for the fourth time that day at 2.00 p.m. and was adjourned after two minutes for half an hour. Again, there was a disruption and it was adjourned until 5.00 p.m. The House met for the sixth and the last time at 5.00 p.m. This last session, which lasted for only 15 minutes, completed all the listed business for the day, including the adoption of a legislative Bill, without any discussion, in a noisy and disruptive House.

The Parliament followed the decision of the executive, presumably after some behind-the-scenes consultations with selected party leaders. The events of 18–22 March and the subsequent decision to reverse some of the unconventional decisions taken earlier were perhaps a culmination of a process marked by ad hocism and expediency in the functioning of the Parliament.

It may be argued that the primary responsibility for undermining the role of the Parliament lies with a disgruntled Opposition and not with the government. It was the Opposition that was indulging in frequent disruptions in the two Houses and the government had no option but to somehow carry on with the task of running the affairs of the nation. This contention may have some validity, but it does not resolve the issue of the complete subservience of the Parliament to the will of the executive. If Bills can be passed, if Budgets can be approved and if Sessions can be adjourned abruptly, an irresponsible or autocratic government in the future can easily get away with the erosion and even the suspension of the legitimate rights of the people.

THE SILENCES OF THE PARLIAMENT

In addition to approving legislative proposals and other government business, the Parliament is an important forum for the discussion of public issues and public grievances through their representatives. There are regular Question Hours for members to ask questions of their choice concerning different ministries. Ministers are responsible for answering these questions and for taking further action as necessary in light of discussions on Starred Questions. Time is allotted for members to make Special Mentions on issues of importance to their constituents, their states and the country. A member is entitled to propose a short-duration discussion on any matter of public importance. He or she can also move a resolution or a private member's Bill for discussion and approval after completing the necessary formalities for doing so.

Debate on important policy issues is highly useful (for example, on subjects such as the National Rural Employment Guarantee Act, 2005, development problems in the least developed parts of the country and regional cooperation in South-east Asia). The issues raised during the debates also influence the course of policy formulation by the government of the day. This is an important strength of India's democracy as national policies of long-term domestic and international importance, including economic policies, are adopted after careful consideration and broad consensus across the political spectrum. This explains why national policies, once approved by the Parliament after discussion, are seldom reversed despite changes of government.

However, there have been occasions when the silences of the Parliament have been just as loud as the debates on foreign policy, employment and development policy. Generally, the tolerance for deviation from established norms and propriety is most evident when there is a clash of interests among different parties in search of political power after elections (or an adverse judicial verdict). The most conspicuous example of such silences was, of course, during the period of Emergency in 1975-7 when violations of established laws and administrative norms were either tolerated or approved through legislative amendments, including Constitutional amendments.

Fortunately for India's democracy, such occasions have been relatively infrequent. The power of the Parliament to alter the fundamental rights of the people and the 'basic structure' of the Constitution has also been declared invalid by the Supreme Court of India as early as 1973 (during the hearing on the famous Kesavananda Bharati case). It will be recalled that the verdict of the Supreme Court in this case was challenged in 1975 by the government after the imposition of the Emergency. It was argued that the Parliament was 'supreme' and represented the sovereign will of the people. As such, if the people's representatives in the Parliament decided to change a particular law to curb individual freedom or to limit the scope of judicial scrutiny, the judiciary had no right to question whether it was Constitutional or not. After listening to the persuasive arguments of legal luminaries, the

Chief Justice of India decided to dissolve the Bench, and the 'basic structure' doctrine was reaffirmed as an unalienable feature of our Constitution.

The 'basic structure' doctrine has not been challenged or compromised by any party or parties in power after 1975. However, in later years, the silences of the Parliament have become more frequent on several issues of public interest. New state governments have been sworn in even though they did not have a majority in the legislatures. Ordinances have been issued by governments without adequate cause, and prosecution of criminal offenders has been deferred to protect the political interests of some parties or powerful leaders. On such issues of paramount national importance, the Parliament has maintained a silence or has given its approval post facto under the Constitution in case such approval was required (for example, for the imposition of the President's Rule in Bihar in 2005 by ordinance, which was later found to be unconstitutional by the Supreme Court).

Again, fortunately for India, these cases have been exceptional, and despite silences and tolerance of the Parliament, the wrong decisions taken by Constitutional authorities have generally been reversed later after judicial scrutiny. However, some unhealthy precedents have been set and it cannot be taken for granted that these will not be repeated in the future.

In this connection, developments in the state of Bihar, after regular state elections were completed in February 2005, are of particular interest. It will be recalled that the electoral verdict in this case was fractured and no party or combination of parties had a clear majority. This included the ruling Rashtriya Janata Dal (RJD), which had been in power for several years. After considering various options, the then governor of the state was pleased to recommend the imposition of

President's rule without dissolving the assembly. However, after patiently waiting for three months, all of a sudden and without any notice or discussion with different political parties, on 23 May 2005, he felt compelled to recommend that the assembly should be dissolved immediately. The Union Cabinet considered it appropriate to meet late at night and advised the President, who was on a state visit to Moscow, to approve the governor's recommendation during the course of the night itself. According to media reports and other available evidence, the real reason for the hasty action was that legislators belonging to some minority parties had decided, after waiting for three months, to join a coalition of other parties that were opposed to the RJD. As it happened, the RJD was a part of the ruling coalition at the Centre with a number of ministers in the Central Cabinet. The Centre, therefore, had no option but to take the midnight decision to prevent another coalition of parties from taking office in Bihar.

The opposition parties in the state were naturally upset by the Centre's decision and some of the affected legislators decided to file a case against it. In defence of its case, an affidavit was filed by the Central government in the Supreme Court. In its affidavit, the government argued that the Court is not to inquire—it is not concerned with whether any advice was tendered by any minister or Council of Ministers to the President, and if so, what was that advice. That is a matter between the President and his Council of Ministers. In other words, according to the government, the Council of Ministers could advise the President to pass any order (irrespective of its merits); the President had no option but to accept that advice under the Constitution and the Supreme Court had no right to examine whether the action of the executive was legal or not!

After hearing the arguments, in October 2005, the

Supreme Court gave a summary verdict declaring the action of the government to dissolve the Bihar assembly as 'un-Constitutional' and unreasonable. The Court, however, did not order the revival of the old assembly, as fresh elections had already been announced by the Election Commission and were scheduled to take place after a few days. The Court's verdict caused considerable public embarrassment to the government since the decision to dissolve the assembly had been taken by the President at very short notice on the advice of the Union Cabinet. In light of the Supreme Court's verdict, the governor of Bihar tendered his resignation.

When the above events were taking place, the Parliament was in recess. The Monsoon Session of the Parliament was reconvened in the last week of July 2005. As per the provisions of the Constitution, the Ordinance to dissolve the state assembly had to be formally approved by the Parliament. The government moved a Bill to that effect, which was duly approved. Interestingly, after the Supreme Court verdict in October 2005 that the action to dissolve the state assembly was unconstitutional, some parties in the Parliament put forward the view that the Supreme Court in its judgment had exceeded its brief since the Ordinance had already been approved by the Parliament of India! Subsequently, in November 2005, after fresh elections were held, a coalition government was formed by parties that had earlier been denied the right to test their majority on the floor of the assembly.

An even more blatant case of transgression of well-established Constitutional conventions by the governor of a state occurred in March 2005 in the state of Jharkhand. After elections, in Jharkhand also, there was no clear majority among the pre-election allies. However, the opposition parties were able to persuade some other elected members to join them. They were thus able to demonstrate their majority to the governor (with 41 members in a House of 80 members). However, the governor decided to swear-in a government headed by a member of the Union Cabinet, who did not seem to have a clear majority. He was also given a number of days to prove his majority on the floor of the House. The opposition parties that claimed to have a majority were extremely upset by this decision of the governor and filed a writ petition in the Supreme Court challenging the decision. On 9 March 2005, the Court passed an order that inter alia gave directions to the Speaker to extend the state assembly session by a day and to conduct a floor test between the contending political alliances. In light of the Supreme Court's decision, the earlier government formed by the Union minister decided to tender its resignation on the advice of the Central government. An alternative government was then formed by a combination of other parties, which was able to prove its majority on the floor of the House.

The directions of the Supreme Court to the Speaker of the Jharkhand assembly raised a legal storm, as several experts interpreted them as intruding into an area that was within the jurisdiction of the legislature. This view was also endorsed by an Emergent Conference of Presiding Offices of Legislative Bodies of India, which was convened at short notice on 20 March 2005 to deliberate on the Constitutional issues arising from the verdict of the Supreme Court. The presiding officers expressed their concern in no uncertain terms over such orders passed by the courts repeatedly which tend to disturb the delicate balance of power between Judiciary and Legislature and appear to be a transgression into the independence of the Parliamentary System of the Country.

In the Parliament, there was no disapproval of the undemocratic actions of the governor. The concern expressed by presiding officers of the legislative bodies was not about the actions of the governor. It was about the Supreme Court transgressing its jurisdiction in giving directions to the legislature for impartially carrying out the Constitutional provisions in respect of the formation of the government.

The role of state legislatures in defending the provisions of the Constitution, including the procedure for the approval of state Budgets, has become even more perfunctory than that of the Parliament. In some states, the Budget sessions are now held for a few days only and Budgets are passed practically without any discussion. The same is the case in regard to the approval of new laws or legislative amendments proposed by the government. Part of the reason for this state of affairs is the unbridled power of the Opposition to disrupt the House and the pressures of coalition politics. The greater the chaos generated when the House is in session, the greater the publicity. Such publicity is considered to be a major gain for parties, particularly small ones, outside the ruling coalition.

15

ETHICS IN BANKING

Although the subject of 'ethics' in the banking sector is relatively new, a vast amount of academic literature is available on the wider subject of ethics, public policy and economics. The central message of this literature is that what may be considered to be ethical or unethical depends largely on the circumstances and the broader economic and political environment in which a particular policy or operational decision is taken. There are only three definitive conclusions emerging from this vast literature that are independent of the context:

(i) Adherence to the 'Rule of Law' in a democratic society is an essential minimum requirement of ethical behaviour;
(ii) Any measure or policy decision that improves the welfare of some without causing harm to anyone else can be considered to be 'ethical' and
(iii) Public policy by the government in power should be designed to promote the 'greatest good for the greatest number'.

These principles, as principles, are entirely appropriate. However, it is interesting that even these are not fully applicable in autocratic or non-democratic regimes. This was, for example, the case during our Independence struggle. In fact, it was the non-violent defiance rather than adherence to law as laid down by the British (for example, during Gandhi's

Salt March, also known as the Salt Satyagraha and Dandi March) that is generally regarded as having been ethical and profoundly inspirational for the people.

On the whole, in practical terms, it is not necessary to look for a unique or universally valid definition of what is ethical and what is not, particularly in the areas of business, banking or economics. When conflicting policy choices are involved, there can be no unique answer to the question of whether a particular choice is ethical. At the same time, while a unique definition of 'ethics' is not feasible, it is also true that whether a particular action or practice is ethical or otherwise is easy to recognize; an example will illustrate the point.

It is well known that the interest rate on microfinance or credit to borrowers from self-help groups (SHGs) is likely to be higher than the interest rate charged by a scheduled bank for direct lending to its borrowers. At the same time, it is also true that a large number of smaller farmers and poor persons have easier access to microfinance institutions than to the formal organized banking sector. The reasons for the interest rate being higher for loans by SHGs is the higher cost of transactions and the need to reach a wider section of people, particularly in rural areas. There is also no scope for cross-subsidization among borrowers on any significant scale as the bulk of loans are for relatively less well-off persons or enterprises. In this situation, it could be legitimate to take the view that higher interest rates, which may have been considered unethical if charged by a bank to the poor, are not unethical per se in the case of SHGs. Precisely where the dividing line between right and wrong is to be drawn is obviously a matter of judgment and may vary from case to case.

In addition to the definitional issue, another vital issue relating to ethics in banking is whether it can be separated from other sectors of the economy, or for that matter, from the standards of ethical conduct in the society as a whole. In other words, should the norms of ethical conduct in banking be different from, say, norms prevailing in stock markets, the private corporate sector or government administration? Suppose unethical conduct, however defined, in the manufacture of, say, jute bags or in investment in the infrastructure sector is tolerated and accepted, then can bankers who finance these activities be considered unethical?

In principle, ethics in banking and economic transactions are interrelated. However, in practice, there is a genuine difficulty in ensuring ethical behaviour in all sectors of the economy, including politics. There are various pulls and pressures in political life in most countries. If the rules of ethical behaviour in banking were intrinsically dependent on ethical behaviour in politics or, for that matter, in different segments of trade and commerce, a country would likely be faced with an insoluble problem.

Against this background, is there anything further that can be said specifically about ethics in banking? Even after taking all the constraints into account, it is still possible to prescribe some rules of behaviour that will make banking more ethical in developing countries, particularly in those that have an independent judiciary and an accountable administration.

The foremost requirement to make businesses, including banking, more ethical is to insist on standards of accounting and auditing that conform to the best international standards and ensure full financial disclosure. Banks, in particular, deal with other people's money. They are intermediary institutions that have been set up and licenced to accept deposits from the public, most of which are small in magnitude. They lend such deposits to other users and producers for carrying out their business activities, which in turn, are expected to generate employment and growth for the country as a whole.

This intermediary function places a special responsibility on the banking sector. It is of utmost importance to ensure that there is complete transparency in respect of the use of the depositors' money and ensuring the safety of funds.

As the sub-prime crisis in the US and the UK in 2007 demonstrated, non-transparency and non-disclosure of financial obligations are not confined to developing countries. For all countries, it has become important to regularly revisit banking, auditing and accounting standards and ensure that guidelines in respect of full disclosures of all obligations, including 'off-balance-sheet' items, are being followed.

One important ingredient of review of disclosure and accounting standards is to eliminate the excessive secrecy that prevails in banking operations in many countries. In India, banks enjoy protection in disclosing the identity of borrowers as well as defaulters and rescheduling of outstanding payments. This non-disclosure is further buttressed by the Official Secrets Act, 1923, which protects government ministries and departments from disclosing directions given by them to public-sector banks, regulatory authorities and other financial institutions. There seems to be no strong reason why names and amounts lent by banks to individual borrowers should not be disclosed and why even defaulters should enjoy the benefits of secrecy provisions.

The rationale for further reducing the scope of secrecy provisions is to ensure that actions taken by banks conform to normally accepted banking and regulatory guidelines and are not unethical—at least on the face of it. Public disclosure would also ensure some exercise of caution by banks in their lending operations and in granting benefits to borrowers by way of rescheduling, and so on. All such operations should not only be reasonable but also be perceived to be so by the general public.

In respect of the responsibility of the Board of Directors for ensuring ethical conduct, the UK amended the Companies Act (with effect from 1 October 2007). In line with similar amendments made in the US (under the Sarbanes-Oxley Act of 2002), the Companies Act in the UK specifically lays down the following seven statutory duties of directors of companies:

(i) Duty to act within prescribed powers;
(ii) Duty to promote the success of the company;
(iii) Duty to exercise independent judgment;
(iv) Duty to exercise reasonable care, skill and diligence;
(v) Duty to avoid conflicts of interest;
(vi) Duty to not accept direct or indirect benefits from others and
(vii) Duty to declare an interest in proposed transactions or agreements.

Similar principles of conduct are also implied in various provisions contained in company laws or contract laws in India. However, in practice, observance of these principles is generally neglected, as the duties of directors are considered to be essentially confined to papers put up by the management. It is desirable to make a distinction between the independent responsibility of directors and the responsibilities of management. Such a move, along the lines of amendments carried out in the UK, would go a long way in ensuring ethical conduct by banks and accountability for decisions taken by them.

A difficult and somewhat thorny issue in regard to regulation and management of the banking sector is the role of politics in determining outcomes. In most developing countries, there is a strong view that banking and financial operations should be conducted to promote growth with equity and special attention should be given to the poorer/ underdeveloped sections of the society in granting access to bank loans. In several countries, including India, there are specific provisions on the quantum of lending that should be directed to persons below the poverty line and other categories of borrowers. Since these provisions are meant to serve the interests of the people, the people's representatives in the Parliament and ministries claim to have a direct role in ensuring that banking operations conform to governmental priorities.

This view has substantial validity and must be respected as an important aspect of democratic accountability in developing countries. However, while ensuring public accountability for banking operations, it is equally important to ensure that political affiliations do not become the primary criterion for the selection of top management or directors in banks. The objective of political neutrality can be met if the same processes are put in place for selection as for the initial appointment of civil servants presently.

In India and several other countries, civil servants are appointed through an open competitive examination process which is conducted by an independent institution, such as the Union Public Service Commission (UPSC). There is no reason why a similar mechanism, at arm's length from the political executive, cannot be set up for the choice of top management and boards of directors in public-sector banks. Selections can be made by an independent statutory commission by inviting applications from qualified professionals and/or through appropriate search committees. The process for selection should be open and well-advertised. As far as private-sector banks and other financial institutions are concerned, it is desirable for the government not to have any role in the selection process.

The point is that while financial priorities and banking policy may be decided at the political level with due accountability, the political executive should not have a direct operational role in the choice of people who run banks and other financial institutions. Such a process should ensure that, while there would always be some exceptions, the management and boards of banks are independent in their functioning and not beholden to a changing political leadership for their appointments.

As is well known, in India, a law has been enacted that grants inalienable rights to the public to seek information from any ministry or public institution on decisions taken by them. This Right to Information (RTI) Act, adopted in 2005, is a momentous step towards opening the governmental decision-making process to public scrutiny. This Act has, over time, led to greater accountability for ethical conduct in banking and other sectors of the economy. There is a strong case for adoption of similar measures to grant legal rights of information to the public in all countries, particularly where governments have a substantial administrative role in the conduct of financial operations.

The sanctity of contracts and redressal of consumer grievances are essential components of a financial system that encourages ethical behaviour by participants. This requires a speedy judicial system where people can go for alleged breach of contract and redressal of their grievances as borrowers or depositors. Unfortunately, in many of the countries, including India, while there is abundance of legislation, there are enormous delays in getting judicial verdicts even in the most blatant cases of breach of contract or illegal behaviour. With a huge backlog of cases in courts at different levels, it often takes more than a decade to get even an initial verdict. In recent years, some initiatives have been taken to encourage the settlement of cases by mutual agreement. However, actual progress in reducing the backlog of cases by using the settlement route has been relatively slow. It goes without saying that, for most ordinary people, justice delayed is justice denied. An important priority—and it goes well beyond the financial sector—is the introduction of measures to reduce delays in the multilayer framework of judicial hearings.

Finally, there can be hardly any doubt that an effective and efficient regulatory system, at the level of the central bank and other supervisory authorities, is essential for furthering the cause of ethics in banking. All countries have central banks and some countries also have additional financial supervisory authorities with designated functions. These agencies are responsible for ensuring compliance with their rules and regulations, thereby encouraging ethical behaviour in dealings between banks and their borrowers and depositors. While rules and regulations as well as periodic inspections are necessary parts of the regulatory framework, the supervisory system in many countries has become overloaded and is also highly bureaucratic and discretionary. A discretionary and inspection-focused system in turn encourages favour-seeking, corruption and other malpractices at the ground level. Rather than relying on inspectors, it would be far more effective if the managements of banks and their boards of directors are made responsible for certifying compliance with applicable rules and regulations. Self-certification, along with statutory obligations of directors for ethical conduct, should ensure that the responsibility for unethical practices cannot be shifted to other agencies or regulators.

While much more needs to be done, these are a few broad principles that can encourage and promote ethical behaviour in banking. These measures are practical and 'doable', and capable of being introduced in the financial sector specifically, even if there are problems in introducing similar principles in non-financial sectors or the economy as a whole.

16

POLITICS AND GOVERNANCE

The state of India's economy, politics and governance, in addition to being important in itself, is also a subject of some contemporary significance in view of a fundamental shift in the structure of the Central government after the General Elections held in May 2014. For the first time since 1989—a quarter of a century ago—we have a government in power constituted by a party that enjoys a majority on its own in the Lok Sabha and is fully accountable to the people for its performance and delivery of public services. From 1989 to 2014, India had as many as nine governments with an average lifespan of about two and a half years. Five of these had a tenure of a year or less with enormous power to allocate resources, control public enterprises and decide interstate allocation of investments. None of these governments could be held accountable for their performance, in view of the so-called 'compulsions of coalition politics'.

By any standards, India's domestic potential is huge. India is a well-established democracy which grants full freedom to its people to do what they wish and provides them with adequate powers to hold the government responsible for its performance. Unlike many other developing countries, India's domestic savings are high and dependence on aid and capital inflows from abroad relatively low. India's economy has also been considerably liberalized since the 1980s, particularly after 1991. India has full access to world-class technology and skills at comparatively low cost. As it happens, unlike the earlier period, at present foreign exchange reserves are also sufficient to tackle any balance-of-payments pressures that might arise without having to seek assistance from abroad.

While India's opportunities and capabilities are comparatively large, it is also true that actual performance in alleviating poverty and providing minimum essential social services to the people has been relatively low. The best-known and internationally recognized measure of socio-economic progress is the HDI, which is computed annually by the UNDP. The HDI is a composite of several basic components of human development, such as life expectancy, literacy, standard of living and health. It is believed to be a more comprehensive measure of progress than per capita income or GDP.

On the HDI index, in 2018, India's rank was 130 among 189 countries globally. In other words, it ranked close to the bottom one-third of countries in terms of human development, notwithstanding the fact that in terms of overall growth rate of the GDP, India was among the fastest-growing developing countries in the world for nearly three decades since the 1980s. India was also the lowest-performing country in respect of HDI among the so-called BRICS nations (that is, Brazil, Russia, India, China and South Africa) in all categories (with the exception of life expectancy, which was somewhat lower in South Africa).

Why this sharp and persistent 'disjuncture' between growth and human development, notwithstanding the universally acclaimed economic reforms of 1991? Growth and reforms are obviously not ends in themselves, particularly in a vibrant democracy 'of the people, by the people and for the people' like India's. High growth and reforms are 'means' to achieve the ends of providing the basic components of human development, especially nutrition, healthcare and literacy, to the people, irrespective of their levels of income. And, this is where India's past performance has been well below the expectations of the founding fathers of the Constitution. It is also symptomatic of the persistent failure of India's system of 'governance' at the highest levels of government and bureaucracy.

So far as economic reforms per se are concerned, there has already been a fair amount of consensus about what needs to be done. Government, at the highest levels, has also announced a large package of reforms in order to boost investor confidence and growth. Some important measures, which are still awaiting full implementation, include interstate GST, land reforms, completion of existing public projects (such as in the power sector or roads and schemes like the Pradhan Mantri Jan Dhan Yojana [PMJDY], to provide benefits to the people). All these proposed economic reforms will certainly contribute to higher growth as and when implemented and hopefully reduce poverty. Ultimately, the main task is to implement what has been promised.

In this context, some of the political and governance issues that also require urgent attention are reforms to promote higher growth combined with poverty alleviation and the availability of essential public services to the people, as promised. India has reasons to be proud of what it has been able to achieve as the world's largest democracy. At the same time, in the working of India's politics and governance, there have been certain developments that have had unintended consequences and that were not visualized when the Constitution was framed.

It hardly needs to be emphasized that a fundamental 'systemic' change, which dominated the working of India's politics until the 2014 elections, was the emergence of coalitions as a 'regular' form of government after 1989. Under the present Constitutional provisions, as a consequence of amendments carried out in 1985 and again in 2003 to prevent defections, there is also a built-in perverse incentive for fragmentation of political parties, particularly at the state level. This is because the smaller a party, the greater the ability of an individual legislator to defect to another party in search of political power. Thus, for example, a member elected from a large national party has very little discretion to defect without the support of a substantial number of other members, who also wish to defect. In a situation where multiparty coalitions are the norm, all regional or caste leaders with a handful of constituencies naturally have a much greater incentive to form their own separate parties rather than join a large single party.

In order to reduce the present built-in incentive for fragmentation of parties and improve governance, it is of utmost importance that the anti-defection law be made applicable to all parties and the so-called independent members who choose to join a government in power. In other words, those parties that join a pre-election or post-election coalition should not be able to defect without having to seek re-election. Such an amendment to the 'anti-defection law' will go a long way in strengthening the principle of collective responsibility of the Cabinet to the people, as enshrined in the Constitution.

A related urgent political reform is to reduce the attractiveness of politics as a career choice to persons with criminal records. According to the statistical survey of elections to the Lok Sabha in 2014, nearly 20 per cent of the candidates surveyed, cutting across party lines (excluding independent candidates), had criminal antecedents. In the Lok Sabha, which has 543 seats in all, well over 100 members had criminal cases pending against them.

The present incentive for persons who have criminal cases

pending in higher courts of appeal (either the High Court or the Supreme Court) should be effectively reversed by giving such cases highest priority if the concerned person is actually elected to the Parliament or a state legislature. Their 'presumed' innocence should be proved within six months of election before they can take their seats in the Assembly or the Parliament. Fast settlement of such cases would provide a big relief to persons with criminal charges who are actually innocent, and not only 'presumed' to be so. And those who are actually guilty may choose not to contest elections so that they are in a position to delay hearings through normal legal procedures!

Another development that has gathered further momentum in recent years is the politicization of India's bureaucracy. In theory, under the Indian system of executive responsibility, there is supposed to be a clear division of the roles between the permanent civil service and the political leadership. The government's policy priorities and its work programme are set by politicians. However, bureaucracy is supposed to ensure that implementation of the approved programme is done according to the laws and procedures in force, without fear or favour, for the benefit of all the people regardless of their political affiliations.

Over the years, slowly but surely, the role of the bureaucracy has been seriously compromised. Any party that comes to power is inclined to appoint favoured bureaucrats in sensitive positions who, in turn, are expected to carry out the wishes of its party leaders, irrespective of their merits or legality. As a result of frequent transfers, administration has naturally become weak. What is even worse is that civil servants, instead of being independent of political leaders or parties in power, have now become subservient to them.

In view of the growing political corruption and

administrative apathy, it is no wonder that India has one of the worst rankings in the Corruption Perceptions Index (CPI) and Global Corruption Barometer compiled by Transparency International. In the 2018 perception index, India's score was 41 on a scale of zero to 100 where zero indicates highly corrupt and 100 stands for very clean.

On the whole, in the past few years, there has been growing disjuncture between economics on the one hand and governance and politics on the other. In the future, the overarching issue that India faces is whether in the years to come, it will be able to resolve what can perhaps be described as public–private dichotomy in the functioning of the country. It is a striking fact that economic renewal and positive growth impulses are occurring largely outside the governmental sector at the levels of private corporations, autonomous institutions and individuals at the top of their professions in India and abroad.

Can something be done to resolve this dichotomy and improve the functioning of politics and governmental system? Although a number of highly positive and encouraging announcements have been made by present as well as several previous governments to improve growth and governance, further strong action is necessary if India is to realize its full potential as an emerging power. Some of the priorities are briefly mentioned below:

(i) Within the framework of the parliamentary form of government, an important priority is to further reduce the political role of the government in the economy, particularly the power of multiple ministries and governments at the Centre and states over public-sector enterprises. Privatization is not the only answer. The real question is whether India can create an 'arm's-length' relationship between the government and these enterprises (that is, the Election Commission, which gives India the largest free and fair elections in human history or for that matter, UPSC-type arrangement, where civil servants are appointed through an open and competitive exam).

(ii) There is also the need to change the distribution of powers between the Union and states under Articles 245 to 255 of the Constitution. It will be desirable to give states exclusive economic powers, for example, in respect of multiple poverty-alleviation schemes and implementation of infrastructure projects.

(iii) The issue of state funding of elections has also been considered from time to time but has not been found acceptable. Not that state funding would eliminate corruption, but with high cost of elections, the lack of it has become an important defence of corruption in the exercise of political and administrative powers. In a budget of several thousands of crores at the Centre and state levels, even an allocation of 0.5 per cent of the budget for elections would generate sufficient resources to provide state funding for defined campaign activities, such as travel in constituencies, discussions or addresses to constituents and party meetings.

(iv) Finally, as mentioned, separation of powers between civil services and ministers for carrying out administrative functions is essential. Greater empowerment of the civil services must, of course, go hand in hand with greater accountability of civil services for their performance and ethical conduct.

There is, of course, a lot more to be done to tackle the challenges of the future. The overarching points for urgent implementation are really twofold. First, the growth of GDP is certainly important and India must do all that is needed to put it on a high growth trajectory. At the same time, high growth is not an end in itself. It must be ensured that the benefits of growth reach all the people, particularly the disadvantaged sections of the society. Second, in order to achieve this objective, reforms have to be broad-based. Highest priority has to be given to enforce collective accountability of government ministries at the Centre and states, combined with administrative reforms to devolve powers to the states for implementation of Central schemes, reduce corruption, simplify rules and facilitate easy access of citizens to public services. India today has the capacity to achieve its full potential as an emerging global power, provided it has the necessary will and determination. The innate ability of the people is immense and has been demonstrated beyond reasonable doubt.

17

THE PROSPERITY PARADOX

The persistence and depth of poverty in India during the colonial period has been recorded, in some detail, by economic historians. In the second half of the nineteenth century and the first half of the twentieth century, poverty took the form of a series of famines that ravaged all parts of India and resulted in the deaths of more than 30 million people. Epidemics and disease were also common, and at the time of Independence, the life expectancy of an average Indian was a mere 32 years. There was no water supply system in the villages and the supply of electricity in the rural areas was unknown. The vast majority of Indians had no access to education or employment. Per capita availability of food actually declined during the 30-year period prior to Independence (1911–41) by as much as 29 per cent.

After Independence, an overriding priority of the national government, as it has been of all governments since then, was to expand physical facilities to provide basic social services such as education, healthcare and nutrition to all sections of the people, particularly the poor. Over the years, physical infrastructure in terms of schools, primary healthcare centres and other facilities has expanded enormously, and a variety of social and anti-poverty programmes have been introduced. An effort has also been made to improve the design of these programmes in light of past experiences and to make social policies more responsive to the needs of the poor. There is also no doubt that the access of the poor to social services has improved after Independence, and an average Indian is significantly better off than he or she would be 30 or 40 years ago. However, a number of studies and field surveys have also revealed significant weaknesses in the implementation of several such programmes. Despite the weakness of statistical data, one finding that stands out is that the poor generally have lower access to public social services than the not-so-poor sections of the society. For example:

(i) Despite substantial expansion of the PDS for food, and an increase in the availability of foodgrains, the proportion of the population whose income is not sufficient to buy the recommended daily level of intake has remained constant, at around 50 per cent.

(ii) The purchase of food by the poor from the PDS is relatively small, particularly in states with the highest concentrations of poverty.

(iii) Poor educational and economic background of parents is a major cause of children dropping out of schools. The incidence of illiteracy among the poor, as a result, continues to be considerably higher than the national average in both urban and rural areas. Public schools in poor urban areas are generally worst equipped in terms of basic facilities such as drinking water or the number of teachers.

(iv) In the case of social assistance schemes such as old-age pension, the identification of beneficiaries has been influenced by considerations other than poverty and the non-poor seem to have benefited more than the poor.

(v) Owing to a paucity of resources, most social programmes are too thinly spread and fragmented to meet the needs of the poor. Bureaucratic functioning and the social distance of government servants from the truly poor are further impediments.

Given the large base of the poor in India, it is obvious that people's access to social services, and the poor's access in particular, cannot be improved without increasing social expenditure substantially. The expenditure on social services by the Centre and states remained around 6 per cent of the GDP from 2012 to 2016. There is certainly scope for improving the efficiency of social programmes. Much more needs to be done to target these programmes better, and reduce the weight of the bureaucracy. However, such improvements will not alter the current picture significantly unless the reach of these programmes is expanded. When public services are scarce and free, they are likely to be pre-empted by the non-poor.

In addition to the need to increase social expenditures while at the same time reducing fiscal deficits, there are three general principles that should be observed in the organization of social services for the poor. First, there is a need to 'prioritize'. Most developing countries tend to allocate a higher proportion of their meagre resources to provide services that benefit relatively few. Thus, for example, in several developing countries, including India, more is spent on higher education than on primary education. Similarly, more resources are devoted to running speciality hospitals than to, say, overcoming vitamin and mineral deficiency among the millions of poor. All countries need facilities for higher education and for specialized treatment of diseases, which also deserve public support. The issue is one of relative proportion of resources devoted to meeting competing ends. It is not equitable for the government to provide subsidies to cover the entire cost of expensive services for a few people. As a principle, all such publicly supported facilities should be encouraged to cover at least a part of their revenue expenditure through charges and fees (with appropriate waivers for those who are unable to pay). In any case, subsidies should be transparent and explicit. The cost of these subsidies should be calculated in per capita terms and periodically published for the information of the public.

A second principle that should be applicable for all services, including those meant for the poor, is the levy of a reasonable fee, which can be waived by the local provider of these services in cases where beneficiaries are unable to pay. There is some evidence that in fee-paying institutions, provided that facilities are adequate, those who can afford to pay are in fact willing to pay. Even partial cost recovery in this manner will improve the quality of services without discriminating against the poor. An alternative scheme that is now being tried out in some industrial and developing countries is to give vouchers to poor families for certain services, which can be used to pay for these services at any public or private facility that accepts them. The providers of services are encouraged to levy charges that cover their full costs, but they have to compete for clients on the strength of the quality of their services. The public cost of supporting these services is reduced as vouchers are given only to poor families by local authorities.

There is now sufficient international experience, including from India, to show that involvement of local NGOs in the provision of basic services for the poor can improve their availability as well as quality. NGOs are already active in several fields, particularly education. A number of them, including those in the field of healthcare, have also earned international reputation for their effectiveness. The main advantage of NGOs in providing basic services is a higher level of motivation and the elimination of indifferent government officials from the process of delivery. Governments, Central and state, would do well to channel as much of their social expenditure as possible through local NGOs. The NGOs should be subject to periodic financial and performance audits, the results of which should be published locally.

Three priority areas of great social and economic importance are: food, literacy and healthcare. Some of the issues in these sectors are briefly discussed below.

THE FOOD SITUATION

From an economic point of view, there is nothing more vital than adequate availability of food. The supply and price of food are also directly linked to the question of poverty in India. The poor spend the bulk of their income on food, and an increase in its price or a reduction in its availability immediately raises the poverty ratio. Food is also a major factor in determining the course of inflation in the economy. It accounts for as much as 46 per cent of the Consumer Price Index (CPI) weightage. As the wages of government and public-sector employees as well as employees in the organized private sector are linked to the CPI, the trend in the price of food directly affects the fiscal and broader economic outlook in the country. For all these reasons, self-sufficiency in food production and active intervention in the market for food have been important elements of India's agricultural policy since the mid-1960s.

In the area of food security, distribution of food is as important as its production. Despite sharp reductions in food supply, India was able to avoid famines in the worst drought years of 1965-6, 1973, 1979 and 1987 because of effective food distribution policies. These made it possible for the affected sections of the population to have access to food despite overall scarcity. The PDS organized through fair price shops and public procurement of foodgrains played a vital role in ensuring access to food.

A legitimate criticism of the PDS is that its reach has been largely confined to the urban areas. Except in times of emergency or drought, the poor in the rural areas are largely dependent on private markets for meeting their requirements of food. Food prices in the rural markets are often higher and the government's procurement operations put further pressure on the rates. In recent years, efforts have been made to 'revamp' the PDS and extend its coverage to tribal, hill and arid areas. This has corrected the urban bias of the PDS, but its coverage still remains regionally uneven. In several states with large concentrations of poverty, the poor's consumption from the PDS is still relatively low.

In the foreseeable future, until such time as the dependence of food production on the monsoon is further reduced, India will need to continue with the policy of holding sizeable stocks of foodgrains. However, in light of changes that have taken place in recent years in the cost of holding stocks and other parameters, there is a strong case for substantially reducing the average level of buffer stocks held by the government. In recent years, procurement, distribution and holding costs have risen sharply partly because of a rise in interest costs and partly because of the 'diseconomies' associated with the large scale of public operations in foodgrains. As procurement prices have become more attractive and more gain is offered to public agencies during the immediate post-harvest period, the peak marketing period is becoming shorter and market arrivals are becoming increasingly concentrated.

An important recent development is the high level of India's foreign exchange reserves, which makes it possible to import food from world markets in times of necessity without depending on the goodwill of other countries or institutions.

India should explore the possibility of entering into long-term options and contracts that guarantee availability of specified quantities of food at prices that are determined according to an agreed formula. These options and contracts should themselves be tradeable, so that actual imports—and exports—can take place depending on the state of domestic production.

EDUCATION FOR ALL

Literature on the development issues of the 1950s and 1960s generally ignored the importance of education and training as factors in promoting economic growth. It was believed that physical capital was crucial to economic growth, and countries that encouraged capital formation in machines and plants were likely to grow more rapidly.

Recent theoretical and empirical research has, in contrast, given prime importance to education and literacy, particularly among females, as key factors in explaining differences in economic performance among developing countries. Cross-country comparisons have indicated that a substantial proportion of growth rate of an economy could be attributed to increases in educational levels of the labour force. While there are differing explanations of the precise ways in which education affects growth, it is generally believed that there are important externalities associated with education, which increases productivity of labour and enhances the rate of technological change in the economy as a whole.

At the time of Independence, almost 12 per cent of India's population was literate and only one child out of three was enrolled in primary school. Since then, there has been significant progress in increasing literacy rates and in expanding the reach of the elementary education system.

Literacy rates have increased from 18.33 per cent in 1951 to 52.21 per cent in 1991 and 74.04 per cent according to the 2011 census. This record is impressive in view of the low initial levels of literacy. The spread of literacy becomes easier as the average population becomes more literate and the incidence of illiteracy among adults and parents decreases. The accessibility of schools in the rural areas has also improved, as nearly 95 per cent of the rural population now has access to schools within a walking distance.

HEALTH SERVICES FOR THE POOR

From a public policy point of view, a principal issue in healthcare is that of equity. The question of equitable access to publicly financed healthcare facilities assumes particular importance in poor developing countries in view of inadequate availability of services, high per capita cost and severe limitation of resources. The experience of most developing countries is that access to public healthcare services is largely confined to better-off sections of the people in urban areas. Similarly, most developing countries tend to spend more on curative care in expensive hospitals with a limited number of beds than on preventive care. Expenditure on preventive care is believed to be more cost-effective as per capita cost of providing such care is generally very low.

Adequate funding is necessary, but it is not a sufficient condition for delivery of healthcare services to the poor. The organization and institutional structure of health services in India suffer from myriad problems—some of which are unavoidable in a country of India's size and diversity. Widespread poverty, illiteracy, lack of rural infrastructure and scarcity of trained medical personnel willing to work in rural areas constitute obstacles to the organization of cost-effective and high-quality public services. Nevertheless, there are some problems that can be resolved in light of past experience in organizing social services on a large scale.

The most important organizational reform that deserves to be implemented is to decentralize delivery of government health services. Decentralization is potentially the most important force for improving efficiency and responding to local health conditions and demands. In India, while local bodies in some states have been given significant authority for managerial services and implementing national programmes, they have practically no financial control/authority (except in some large cities). Transfers from states to local authorities for expenditure on programmes are also limited. The bulk of these transfers are specific-purpose transfers to cover fixed expenditure, such as staff salaries.

Centralization of financial powers is a major hurdle in making health services more responsive to local conditions and local needs. It is also a major cause of delay and inefficiency as even the slightest deviation in specification of drugs or service requires approval of a number of departments, with several layers of bureaucracy, at state headquarters. Decentralization of financial powers, with appropriate audit requirements and performance monitoring, can contribute greatly to improving the quality of healthcare in rural areas and strengthening accountability of local institutions. It should also facilitate greater participation by the community, through NGOs, in the health sector. Experience shows that the involvement of NGOs at the local level can be an effective instrument of improving public awareness of health programmes, and of making primary and community health centres more accountable.

To conclude, India's record in improving the socio-economic well-being of its people has fallen short of the targets set out in the earlier Five-Year Plans. It also compares unfavourably with the average performance of developing countries as a whole. Fast-growing developing countries have, of course, done considerably better than the average, and have succeeded in virtually eliminating illiteracy and substantially reducing infant mortality and malnutrition. In improving access and delivery of social services to the poor, India faces obstacles arising from administrative bottlenecks and financial stringency. In view of the rising burden of public debt and the growth of administrative expenditure, resources available for investment in social sectors have become constrained. There is little hope of improvement in socio-economic indicators unless public expenditure priorities are reconsidered and altered in favour of social sectors. There is no social or economic justification for continuing with non-essential subsidies and investments in bankrupt public enterprises. The poor are hurt more than the rich by these problems. A high growth rate of the economy should help in increasing the availability of public resources for investment in social sectors. Further, data for India as well as other developing countries shows that, within particular regions and states, enrolment ratios in respect of elementary education and demand for primary health services increase with per capita household income. These demand-side effects, combined with better implementation of announced policies, partly explain why some developing economies do better in human development than India.

18
THE FUTURE IS OURS

This book is being published after the Lok Sabha elections held in May 2019. The previous government has been re-elected for a second five-year term (2019–24) with a substantial majority. In its first term, the government had already launched several important reforms such as GST, which, despite some hiccups, is one of the most significant reforms in India's economic history. Several other positive measures were also taken: disbursement of subsidies to the poor through DBT; significant increase in public investment in infrastructure and foreign investment inflows; labour reforms and launch of the 'Digital India' campaign. Before elections in May 2019, the government had also directed all departments to come up with a '100-day plan' listing all the suggestions and reforms that could be implemented over the next three months. Soon after the elections, the government also announced a long list of policy measures, including consolidation of public-sector banks, which different ministries have been directed to launch.

In the next few months, a major task for the present government is to review the actual implementation of several of these schemes in the states and districts. On the economic front, an urgent priority is to ensure creation of jobs in both the unorganized and the organized sectors to accelerate growth and to improve the functioning of the financial sector as soon as possible by reducing the timeline for enforcing policies announced in respect of the Insolvency and Bankruptcy Code 2016.

There are also some other economic issues that need to be handled by the government as early as possible. The stagnation of exports and the failure of the manufacturing initiatives in the previous few months need to be addressed. Agriculture needs special attention, and an important challenge is how best to deal with the growing surpluses that have reduced farmers' income. In May 2019, unemployment in the labour force was more than 7 per cent, which was higher than the last several decades.

There are also a number of long-term reforms that may be initiated in the next few months, but their implementation may take two to three years before the full benefits are realized. In handling some of these long-term issues, one great advantage that India has is that its economic fundamentals are very strong, perhaps better than in the past 30 years. Looking ahead, an important reform for realizing India's full economic potential is to further simplify administrative procedures and reduce the number of agencies, at different levels, involved in providing clearances for undertaking any activity. In May 2019, at least 30 different clearances, involving several agencies at the Centre and states, were required for setting up even a modest-sized industrial factory.

After the elections, the government has also announced its intention to introduce a programme in respect of 'ease of doing business' by corporates and public-sector agencies. This is a positive initiative. However, what has been announced is not enough. As mentioned in the earlier chapters, there are a number of other governance and political issues that need to be handled by the government as early as feasible. Some of these are highlighted here. First, there is a need to drastically simplify the governance system at the bureaucratic level.

With the exception of selected areas where strict timelines can be prescribed for giving approvals (such as in the case of forest and environment clearances), it is desirable to cut through the elaborate red tape and rely primarily on 'self-certification'. The government can lay down standards and norms (for example, in respect of pollution or fire safety) and the entity concerned may be required to 'self-certify' at the highest levels of management that these have been complied with in accordance with the notified procedures. Government agencies can make random checks and in case there are clear-cut violations, appropriate penal action can be taken. Similarly, the present complexity in regulations should be reduced drastically. Such simplification has been tried out in some areas with success (for example, with regard to foreign exchange transactions).

A related area, at the Centre as well as states, is transparency in the decision-making process within the government. A major step towards achieving this has been taken with the enactment of the RTI Act in 2005. A further step in this direction should be to make it mandatory for all the ministries and the departments of the government to voluntarily make information on the decisions taken by them available to the public (excluding security-related subjects, of course). If this can be done, the free media and the civil society institutions will constitute an effective instrument for enforcing accountability in the government's decision-making process.

Case studies of international experience in the management of public services show that the objective of such programmes can be achieved better and at a lesser cost if a distinction is made between the ownership (by the government) and the delivery (by NGOs and local enterprises) of such services. In such cases, the public authorities retain the responsibility for regulating and monitoring the activities, providing subsidies where necessary and laying down distribution guidelines.

These suggestions for redefining the role of the government in the economy are by no means exhaustive or permanent. The role of the government in the economy should be kept under continuous review and it should evolve as necessary for the benefit of the people as a whole.

It is also desirable to reduce the political powers of ministers and their vested interests in the allocation of public resources. A minister, as the political head of a ministry, enjoys enormous executive powers. Part of the rationale for entrusting politically appointed ministers, of whom several have very little previous administrative experience, is that the ministry is supposed to be accountable to the Cabinet and to the Parliament through them.

While the above system is sound in principle, in practice there has been substantial erosion in the ability of the Parliament/legislatures to hold ministers responsible, either collectively or individually, for the decisions taken by them on behalf of their ministries. In addition to the principle of collective responsibility (which shields ministers from taking individual responsibility), another reason why ministers are not held accountable is that most subjects of direct interest to the public in the economic area are in the Concurrent or State Lists of business. The Central ministers are free to make pronouncements, approve policy guidelines and set all-India targets, but the actual implementation of many programmes is in the hands of individual states. A familiar excuse given by Central ministers for their failure in meeting the targets announced by them is that the states are responsible, not the Centre. The states, on the other hand, blame the Centre for the inadequate allocation of funds, inappropriate guidelines or approval delays by one or more ministries at the Centre.

An important political priority for the future is to ensure that whatever annual targets are announced by a ministry (in consultation with other concerned ministries) are carefully reviewed for their feasibility in implementation. Once an annual target is announced by a ministry, it should have full authority to implement it and it should be the ministry itself that is held accountable for the actual performance. If there is a change of ministers during the course of the year, then the new minister must once again affirm or change the target with the approval of the Parliament.

India has some highly distinguished public institutions such as the Election Commission, the Central Information Commission and the UPSC, which have rendered excellent service to the country. Appointments to these institutions are made by the government. However, once appointed, the members have full authority to carry out the task assigned to them without any interference or approval by the concerned ministries. Similar autonomous institutions should be created for the allocation of all valuable national resources, including oil and gas. The government, even at the highest level, should refrain from giving directions to such institutions. If necessary, the Parliament should adopt a resolution to this effect.

In order to simplify the administrative procedure, it is also essential to reduce the large number of persons who are hired as civil servants across a large number of ministries at different levels and in several departments to design, coordinate and implement similar policies. At present, there is a built-in reluctance to simplify administrative procedures as, over time, this may lead to a large number of staff members with nothing much to do in their existing offices. To overcome this problem, while simplifying procedures, the government should also introduce an 'early retirement scheme', which would permit members of staff who do not have sufficient office work to retire if they wish to do so earlier than their pre-scheduled date.

A further measure for the greater empowerment of civil service personnel, while reducing their number over time, is to reform the procedure for launching vigilance inquiries and the number of agencies involved in such investigations. The ease with which investigations can be launched without adequate cause and then closed after several years for lack of evidence is a major cause of harassment and pain for honest civil servants at higher levels. Civil servants often avoid taking a decision, according to the rules in place, on a financial or controversial matter without seeking ministerial approval. It is feared that doing so would lead to an inquiry at the insistence of a minister or a business group who will be adversely affected by that decision. The fear of taking decisions is a major cause of delays and atrophy in the decision-making process.

The basic issue that needs to be tackled to improve the morale of civil servants is that of the 'separation of powers' within the executive—between ministers and civil servants—in so far as postings, transfers, promotions and other similar administrative matters are concerned. The separation of powers among the three branches of the government—the executive, the legislature and the judiciary—is already enshrined in the Constitution. Although there has been considerable encroachment by the executive into legislative and even judicial areas, it can still be said that these three separate branches enjoy a substantial measure of autonomy and independence (if they wish to exercise it). Within the executive branch, however, the civil service is now completely dependent on the pleasure of the ministers in regard to even the most mundane and routine administrative matters. It is essential to revert to a rule-based system of administration, which circumscribes the powers of politicians and confers greater authority on the civil service itself, for self-regulation.

Under the present constitutional provisions, as a consequence of amendments carried out in 1985 and again in 2003 to prevent defections, there is also a built-in perverse incentive for the fragmentation of political parties at the time of election. This is because the smaller a party, the greater the ability of an individual legislator to defect to another party in search of political power. Thus, for example, a member elected from a large national party has very little reason to defect without the support of a substantial number of other members who also wish to defect. However, if the same person is a member of a small party of five or 10 members, a consensus to defect among all of them, or even only three or four of them—and then switch from one coalition to another—is easier to achieve. The same is true of the so-called 'independent' members who are supported by some political parties during elections. In a situation where multiparty coalitions are the norm, all regional or caste leaders with a handful of constituencies naturally have a much greater incentive to form their own separate parties rather than join a large party. In the Lok Sabha, with 543 members, a party with, say, 10 or 15 members (or even less) can join the government, enjoy ministerial berths and then delay, or help, in amending a cabinet decision on an important policy measure. Similarly, a party with even three or four seats can join the government and choose the portfolio that it wishes for. If things don't work out, any small party or a combination of such parties can threaten to leave the government and destabilize it (in case it does not have a large majority).

In order to reduce the present built-in incentive for the fragmentation of parties and to improve governance in the future, it is of utmost importance that the anti-defection law be made applicable to all parties and the so-called independent members who *choose* to join a government in power. In other words, parties that join a government should not be able to defect without having to seek re-election. Such an amendment to the 'anti-defection law' will go a long way in strengthening the principle of collective responsibility of the Cabinet to the people, as enshrined in the Constitution.

Another important priority for the future is to redefine the primary role of the government in the economy. This is a difficult issue, as the government is directly responsible for initiating political and economic reforms for the people in order to alleviate poverty and accelerate India's growth as a global emerging power. Nevertheless, as it happens, despite some important measures to liberalize domestic and international control in respect of production, trade and capital flows, India still remains one of the most heavily regulated economies in the world. In fact, over time, despite liberalization, the role of the government (including state governments) has expanded practically in all spheres of the economy.

Over time, the number of ministries and departments involved in regulating almost all segments of the economy, society, foreign affairs, defence and border security have expanded enormously. In addition to the traditional ministries such as Finance, Defence, Home, Commerce and Industry, etc., we now also have more specialized ministries such as Micro, Small and Medium Enterprises (MSMEs); Jal Shakti; Animal Husbandry, Dairying and Fisheries; Labour and Employment; Skill Development and Entrepreneurship; AYUSH (Ayurveda, Yoga and Naturopathy, Unani, Siddha and Homoeopathy); Culture; Tourism; Social Justice and Empowerment; Youth Affairs and Sports; and so on. In 2019, in the second term of the present government, as many as 57 Cabinet ministers, ministers of state (with independent charge) and other ministers were appointed. As in the past, it is likely that the total number of ministers in the government will be further increased after some time. All the announced policies that different ministries handle, in association with other concerned ministries with similar roles, naturally take a long time to be implemented on the ground, particularly in rural and underdeveloped areas of the country.

In 2019 and beyond, with a significant majority in its second term, at the macroeconomic level, the political (that is, ministerial) role of the government should be to ensure a stable and competitive environment with a strong external sector and a transparent domestic administrative system. While the macroeconomic priorities (for example, the so-called trade-off between growth and inflation) may be decided by the government, the instrumentalities for achieving these objectives must be left to autonomous regulatory and promotional agencies. Similarly, the government's direct role in economic areas should be reset in favour of ensuring the availability of public goods (such as roads and water supply) and essential services (such as healthcare and education) to the people. In these areas, the government's role must expand substantially. At the same time, its role in managing commercial enterprises deserves to be correspondingly reduced.

This is a relatively short list of agendas for the future for the re-elected government. Much more can, of course, be done to realize India's full economic potential as one of the fastest-growing developing countries. If, over the next three to four years, India is able to introduce the above non-controversial reforms in its economical and governance structure, these will definitely have a major positive impact on India's growth as well as poverty alleviation in the future.

INDEX

Actual User Policy, 97
Adjustment programme, 80–81
Administrative ability, 19
After-tax profit, 36
Agricultural credit, 124
Agriculture
    accelerated growth, 74–75
    foodgrains production, 74
    growth in electricity
    consumption, 88
    growth of output, 66
    growth rate in, 55, 66
    high-yielding varieties
    (HYVs) of seeds, 74
    improvement in agricultural
    production, 75
    inputs prices, 74
    production base, 74
    redistribution of income
    from, 11
    sharp increase in
    productivity, 86
    support prices of agricultural
    commodities, 75
Agro-based industries, 55
Aid India Consortium, 29
Aid-dependent objectives, 22
'Aid-weariness', period, 30
Animal Husbandry ministry, 200
Annual Survey of Industries
    (ASI), 59

Anti-defection law, 178, 199–200
Anti-inflation policy, 77
Anti-poverty programmes, 183
Arbitrage, 105, 144–46
Asian crisis, 115, 118, 139, 148
    backdrop, 121
    cross-border interbank
    positions, 117
    degree of deviation from
    best practices, 115
    domestic and international
    developments, 118
    external debt, 117
    impact on Indian financial
    markets, 122
    Indian experience, 118–22
    lessons from, 115–18
    paradigmatic shift, 139
'Asian Miracle', 115
Assets and liabilities, risk
    management, 151
AYUSH (Ayurveda, Yoga and
    Naturopathy, Unani,
    Siddha and Homoeopathy)
    ministry, 200

Bad management, 28
Balance-of-payments, 3, 13, 10,
    16, 22–24, 26–27, 29–30, 45,
    63, 67, 80–92, 95–98, 104, 112,
    135, 144, 176

adjustment, 13
crisis, 3, 24, 27, 29, 96, 112, 119
deficit, 23
gain, 45
imbalance, 95
Banking industry
  adherence to 'rule of law', 166
  Basel principles, 121
  competitive conditions, 120
  consumer grievances redressal, 172
  'ethics' in, 166–72
  intermediary function, 169
  protection in disclosing the borrowers identity, 169
  public accountability for operations, 171
  restrictions on exposure to equity, 121
  rules of ethical behaviour, 168
  sanctity of contracts, 172
Below the poverty line, package of services for, 78
Bharat Heavy Electricals Limited (BHEL), 87
Borrowed capital, 33–34
Brazil
  agricultural sector, 14
  automobile manufacturing cost, 7
  industrialization, 5
  inflation, 7
BRICS nations, 176
Budget session, 155–57, 165
Bureaucratic controls, 67

'Calculated volatility', policy, 149
Canalization, 60–61
Capital account liberalization, 116–17
Capital accumulation, 65, 111
Capital flows, 69, 116, 140–41, 145–46, 200
  importance, 140
  primary determinants of exchange rate, 140
Capital gains tax (CGT), 102
Capital goods, 13
Capital-intensive industries, 43
Capital-output ratio, 12, 67, 111
Capital subsidy, 58
Capital tax, idea, 33
Cash subsidies for merchandise exports, 47
Central Information Commission, 197
Centralization of financial powers, 191
China, 176
  growth rate, 66
  trade surpluses, 151
Coalition politics
  compulsions, 175
  pressures, 165
Commercial borrowings, 98–99
Companies Act, 41, 170
Company taxation, higher rate, 39
Competitive strength, 127–30, 132, 134–35
Competitiveness index, 132
'Connected lending', 121
'basic structure' doctrine, 161
Consumer preferences,

importance to, 131
Consumer Price Index (CPI), 187
'Convertibility clause', 61-62
Corporate taxation, 100, 32-33, 41
    base of taxation, 33-35
    effective rates, 36
    minimum rate, 44
    progression in rates, 37
    rate of taxation, 35-42
    tax incentives, 42-44
Corruption Perceptions Index
    (CPI), 180
Corruption, 11, 173, 179, 181-82
Cost of living index, 79
Cost, insurance and freight
    (CIF), 49
Cost-benefit analysis, 18, 54
Cost-consciousness, 19
Credit expansion, 117
Crude oil, increasing domestic
    production, 80
Currency Board, 139

Dairying and Fisheries ministry,
    200
Dandi March, 167
DBT, 193
Debt crises, 27
Debt service obligations,
    rescheduling, 27
Decision-making process,
    transparency in, 195
Declining sterling reserves, 29
Defections, 178, 199
'Demand' situation, 105-7
Depreciation allowance, 42-43
Depreciation, 100, 143, 150
'Development impact', 27

Development paradigm, 111-12,
    117
    change in, 112
Development strategy, 119
Differential tax rates, 39
'Digital India' campaign, 193
Dividend tax, 100
Dividends, compulsory
    declaration, 40
Dollar-rupee transaction, 148
Domestic assets, free
    convertibility, 142-43
Domestic interest rates, 145-46
Domestic savings, 107, 119, 175
Domestic savings rates, 111
Domestic structural constraint,
    67
Double taxation, 39, 100
Drop-out from schools, 184
Dual exchange rate system, 47-48

'Early retirement scheme', 197
'Ease of doing business', 194
East Asian crisis, 113, 115-16
Economic liberalism, 131
Economic management, 67,
    130-31
Economic reforms, 176-77, 200
Education for All, 189-90
'Efficient' public sector, 110
Election Commission, 156-57,
    163, 181, 197
Electoral verdict, 161
Electricity generation, 76
Elimination of aid, 23
Emergency, 160
Employment-oriented
    programme, 18, 57

Employment-oriented strategy, 55
Employment-related subsidies, 58
'Emporia trade', 129
Energy efficiency, 85, 107
Equity investment, 99–100
Essential commodities, shortage, 77
Euromoney, 81
Exchange rate
   adjustment, 17
   expectations, 150
   fluctuations, 151
   policy, 148
   regime, 107, 139
   unification, 47
Excise duties, 101
Export and import projections, 24
Export performance, 67, 106
Export policy, 95–96
   foreign exchange balance sheet, 96
   preferential access to institutional and bank credits, 96
   profitability of industrial exports, 96
   simplification of duty drawback, 96
Export processing zones (EPZs), 50
Export profitability, 106
Export subsidies, 8, 13
Export surplus, 23, 130
Exports, stagnation, 67, 194
Extended Fund facility, 80
External commercial borrowings, 142

External crises (1990s), 151
FDI, xiii, 145, 151
Fertilizer subsidy, 94–95
Finance, 61, 107–8, 111
Finance Bill, 157
Financial crises (1990), 142
Financial intermediaries, 114, 125
   dominated by, 114
   role, 114
Financial markets, liberalization, 125
Financial powers, centralization, 191
'Financial repression', costs, 113
Financial system, 107, 111–13, 116–22, 125–26, 129, 172
Fiscal adjustment, 104
Fiscal deficit, government commitment to reduce, 107
Fiscal incentives, 36, 42
Fiscal policy, 32, 57–58, 106, 108–9
   flexible, 43
   promoting investments, role, 108
Five-Year Plan
   First, 29, 65, 86
   Second, 64–65
   Sixth, 73
Food Corporation of India (FCI), 93
Food policy, 92–93
Food prices in the rural markets, 188
Food security, 187
Foreign aid to India, 30
Foreign collaboration, 109

'Foreign exchange constraint', 26, 94
Foreign institutional investors (FIIs), 145
Forest and environment clearances, 195
Forex markets, 116, 140–41
  appropriate policies, 141
Forward-looking planning, 131

Gandhi, Mahatma, 153, 166
Gates, Bill, 89n1
GDP, 5, 55, 66–68, 73–74, 80, 98, 107, 110, 176, 182, 185
Global Competitiveness Report, 132
Global Corruption Barometer, 180
Government expenditure, slowdown in, 104
Green Revolution, 66
Gross fixed capital formation (GFCF), 86
GST, 177, 193
Gulf crisis, import-compression measures, 104
Gulf War, 105

HDI index, 176
Health services
  decentralization, 191
  organizational reform, 191
'Hedging', 151
Higher income growth, 73–74
Hindustan Steel, 87
Hong Kong
  degree of industrialization, 112

exports of manufactured goods, 14
'100-day plan', 193
IMF, 22, 80–81, 116, 119, 139, 148
Import compression, effects, 104
Import liberalization, 60, 63
Import policy, 59–61, 96–98, 109
  non-priority areas, 97
Import substitution, 4–5, 8–10, 15, 17–18, 21, 24–26, 28, 65, 96–97
Import tariff structure, 97
Incremental capital-output ratio, 67
Incremental wages, 59
World trade share of India, 67
Indian Science and Technology Policy, 83
Indian Science Congress, 84–85
'Indigenous clearance', 59
Indonesia, growth rate, 66
Industrial deregulation, 63
Industrial Development Bank of India, 81
Industrial future, 110
Industrial growth, 8, 15, 54–56, 66, 95, 103, 110
  key to, 110
Industrial licencing,
  dismantling, 130
Industrial policy, 17, 53–54, 58
  expenditure policies, 57
  finance, 61–62
  fiscal policies, 57
  historical experience, 54–57
  import policy, 59–61
  incentives for labour-intensive investment, 58–59,

licencing policies, 57
monetary policies, 57
objectives, 53–54
Industrial production, index, 76, 103
Industrial Revolution, 89
Industrial strength, 130
Industrialization, 3–7, 9, 11, 16–17, 19, 54–55, 57, 65, 67, 112
   of developing countries, 3
   market-oriented patterns, 112
   rapid rate, 6
Inflation, 7, 13, 73–74, 76–77, 92, 106, 108, 125, 135, 146–47, 187
   control, 76–77, 139
Inflow of capital, minimum restrictions on, 120
Infrastructure, 109
   disparity, 135
   improvement in, 76
Insolvency and Bankruptcy Code (2016), 194
Institutional reform, 56, 125
Integrated Rural Development Programme (IRDP), 77
Intellectual Property Rights, 89–90
Inter-corporate
   dividends, 41
   investment, 35, 38, 41–42
Inter-industry relations, 27
Investment allowance, 58, 100, 108
   reintroduction, 100

Jal Shakti ministry, 200
Japan
   domestic interest rates, 146
   per capita growth rate, 112

Kesavananda Bharati case, 160
Korea, exports of manufactured goods, 14

Labour and Employment ministry, 200
Labour-intensive products, 95
Labour-intensive project, 61
Labour subsidy, 13, 17
Labour-surplus economy, 53, 57
Land reforms, 177
Liberal licencing, 50–51
Liberalization of economy, 95
Licencing, virtual abolition, 107
Life expectancy, 86, 176, 183
'Liquidity at risk', 141
'Liquidity squeeze', 104
Literacy rates, 190
Little, Ian, 4
Lok Sabha
   accountability, 175
   statistical survey of 2014 elections, 178
   tainted members, 178

Macroeconomic
   instability, 105
   priorities, 201
   stability, 105
Malaysia, growth rate, 66
Management challenges, 127–30, 132–36
   cost-competitiveness, 134

infrastructure deficiency, 135
international
  competitiveness, 132
openness of the world
  economy, 133
tariff liberalization, 133
Management culture, consumer-
  focused, 131
Manufactured consumption
  goods, 13
Manufacturing capital goods, 87
Manufacturing industries,
  production, 103
Manufacturing initiatives,
  failure, 194
Manufacturing production,
  turning point, 103
Maritime trade, 129
Market-determined strategy of
  development, 111
Market mechanism, reliance
  on, 68
Merchandise exports, cash
  subsidies for, 47
Metals and Minerals Trading
  Corporation (MMTC), 60
Mexico
  agricultural production, 8
  agricultural sector, 14
  balance-of-payments, 9
  crises, 116
  currency convertibility, 8
Micro, Small and Medium
  Enterprises (MSMEs)
  ministry, 200
Ministry of Natural Resources
  and Scientific Research, 84
'Momentum' trading, 150

National Commission to
  Review the working of the
  Constitution, 153
National income, 7, 73
National Planning Committee,
  83
National Rural Employment
  Guarantee Act (2005), 159
National Rural Employment
  Programme (NREP), 77
Natural gas utilization
  for fertilizers and
  petrochemicals, 88
Naxalism, 153-54
'Negative' externalities, 114
Nehru, Jawaharlal, 82-84, 153
New economic policy, 63
Non-banking financial
  companies (NBFCs), 117
Non-performing assets (NPAs),
  122-23
Non-priority areas, investment
  in, 42
NRIs, 46, 47, 48, 50, 51, 104, 145
  cash subsidies, 51
  investment by, 49-52,
    145-46
  remittances, 46-48
  rupee deposits, interest
    rates, 144
  savings deposits, 45, 48-49
  tendency in hoard foreign
    currencies, 46

'Off-balance-sheet' items, 169
'Office of profit', 156
Official Secrets Act (1923), 169
Oil crises, 143

Oil import bill, 80
Organisation for Economic Co-operation and Development (OECD), 4, 106
'Organizational effectiveness', 133

Pakistan
  growth rate of exports of manufactured goods, 14
  investment pattern, 15
  national income, 7
  principal tools of economic policy, 8
  standard of living, 11
Parliament of India
  diminishing role, 153
  ineffective political leadership, 154
  power, 160
  proceedings, 154
  question hours, 159
  silences, 159–65
  time and space allocation, 152
Patent and Designs Act (1911), 89
Patent Laws, 89–90
Patents Act (1970), 89
Per capita income growth, 66
Perception index, 2018, 180
Periodic exchange rate adjustment policy, 16
Pokhran, imposition of sanctions, 143
Political reform, 178
Politicization of Indian bureaucracy, 179

Portfolio investment, 145
  liberalization, 120
Poverty, 3, 56, 171, 176–77, 181, 183–84, 187–88, 190, 200–1
  alleviation, 77–78
  alleviation schemes, 181
  persistence and depth, 183
Pradhan Mantri Jan Dhan Yojana (PMJDY), 177
Price mechanism, allocative efficiency, 18
Pricing of shares, 101–2
Priority areas, 32, 42, 97, 187
Priority for the future, 125, 197, 200
'Process consultants', 88
'Process-design capabilities', 87
'Professionalism' primacy of, 133
Protection against competition, 10
Protectionism, 65
Provident Fund, 59
Public distribution system (PDS), 77, 93, 95, 184, 187–88
  expansion, 184
  legitimate criticism, 188
Public investment, increase in, 106, 193
Public policy, 166
Public-private dichotomy, 180

Quantitative restrictions (QRs), 96–99

Railways, revenue-earning traffic, 73

Rashtriya Janata Dal (RJD), 161–62
'Realistic' exchange rate policy, 25
Red tape, 59, 195
Relief for the common man, 78–79
Rescheduling operations, 27–28
Reserve Bank of India (RBI)
 exchange rate policies, 148–49
 minimum shareholding in the SBI, 123
 periodic credit policy statements, 147
Right to Information (RTI) Act, 172, 195
'Rule of Law', 166
Rules of Procedure and Conduct of Business, 156
Rupee exchange rates, 150
Rural banking, 124
Rural landless employment guarantee programmes, 78
Russia, 14, 29, 115

Salt March, 167
Sarbanes-Oxley Act, 170
Saving mobilization, 34
Schumpeter, Joseph, 89
Science and technology promotion, 79
Scientific policy resolution, 84
 objectives, 84–85
Scitovsky, Tibor, 4
Scott, Maurice, 4
SCs and STs development, 78

scholarships for students, 78
Second World War, 5
Securities and Exchange Commission (SEC), 62
Self-certification, 173, 195
Self-help groups (SHGs), 167
Self-reliance, 20–31, 54, 79
 emphasis on, 31
 formulation of targets, 21
 meaning, 20
 national or international self-sufficiency, 20
 objective, 21
 rescheduling in the context, 28
Self-sufficiency in food, 21, 68, 131, 187
Separation of powers, 181, 198
SHGs, loans by, 167
Singapore, industrialization degree, 112
Skill Development and Entrepreneurship ministry, 200
Social and economic importance, priority areas, 187–92
 education for all, 189–90
 food, 187–89
 health services for the poor, 190–92
Social assistance schemes, 184
Social cost-benefit analysis, 18
'Social equality', 18
Social expenditures, 185
Social Justice and Empowerment ministry, 200

Socio-economic indicators, 192
South Africa, HDI, 176
South Korea, industrialization degree, 112
Soviet Planning model, 64
Soviet trade, collapse of, 106
Soviet Union, collapse of, 105, 112
Special drawing right (SDR), 80
Stabilization programme, 105
Stagnation, 4, 7, 16, 67, 194
Standards of living, 11
State Financial Corporations (SFCs), 61
State funding of elections, 181
State legislatures, role, 165
State policy, objectives, 64
State Trading Corporation (STC), 60
Steel Authority of India Ltd (SAIL), 94
Steel policy, 94
Sub-prime crisis, 169
Supreme Court, 160–65, 179
   Constitutional issues, 164
   directions of the Jharkhand's speaker, 164
   summary verdict, 163

Taiwan
   growth rate, 66
   industrialization degree, 112
   manufactured goods exports, 14
'Tariff jumping', 99
Tariff structure, 8, 15
   rationalization, 15, 17
Tax avoidance, 38, 40

Tax concessions, objectives, 43
'Tax holiday', five-year, 42
Tax incentives, 33, 42–44
Tax inspectors, 11
Taxation Laws (Amendment) Bill (1973), 40
Taxation without representation, 155–59
Technological capabilities trends, 86–88
   capital formation composition, 86
   Indian technological capability, 86–88
Technological development, state's role, 90
Technological revolution, 91
Technology policies, priorities, 85
Thailand, growth rate, 66
Total factor productivity growth, 131
Trade opportunities, 65, 127
Trade-off between growth and inflation, 201
Transparency International, 180
Twenty Point Programme, 77

UK
   domestic interests rates, 146
   sub-prime crises, 169
   Companies Act amendment, 170
'Ultimate' self-reliance, 20
Uncertainty periods, 116
'Under-the-table' payments, 102
Union of Soviet Socialist Republics (USSR), collapse

of rupee trade, 104
Union Public Service
   Commission (UPSC), 171,
   181, 197
'Unity in Diversity', goals, 153
US
   domestic interest rates, 146
   sub-prime crises, 169
   Sarbanes-Oxley Act
   amendment, 170

Water-lifting technology, shift
   in, 88
Watt, James, 89n1
World Bank, 81, 116
World Economic Forum, 132
World Trade Organization
   (WTO) agreement, 133

Youth Affairs and Sports
   ministry, 200